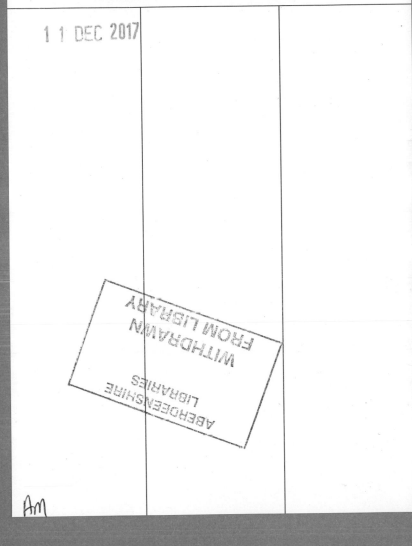

An Otter
On The Aga

An Otter
On The Aga

AND OTHER TRUE TALES
FROM AN ANIMAL SANCTUARY

Illustrations by Rex Harper

Rex Harper

headline
review

First published in 2007
by HEADLINE REVIEW

An imprint of Headline Publishing Group

I

Cataloguing in Publication Data is available from the British Library

ISBN 978 0 7553 1627 4

Typeset in Scala by Avon DataSet Ltd,
Bidford-on-Avon, Warwickshire

Printed and bound in Great Britain by
Mackays of Chatham plc, Chatham, Kent

HEADLINE PUBLISHING GROUP
A division of Hachette Livre UK Ltd
338 Euston Road
London NW1 3BH

www.reviewbooks.co.uk
www.hodderheadline.com

This book is dedicated to all my family but in particular to Julie, who believed in our dream and by sheer determination and hard work made certain that we achieved our goal.

Contents

Acknowledgements

Thanks to Vicky Halls for starting the ball rolling; to Mary Pachnos, Val Hudson and in particular Garry Jenkins for steering me through the last year and for bringing so much interest into my retirement; to all my colleagues in the RSPCA and the veterinary world for their friendship and support; and, most of all, to my family for their willingness to assist me, remembering stories and helping me to understand the world of computers and e-mail. A special mention for my wife Julie, who has shared fifty years of our singular brand of chaos and still seems to enjoy our eccentric lifestyle!

CHAPTER ONE
The Cat With One Eye

I'd barely taken a sip of my morning tea when there was a loud knock at the door. I discovered our local vet, Christopher, standing in the gloom. He was holding a limp and lifeless-looking form, wrapped in a towel.

'Sorry to bother you so early, Rex. I was wondering whether you'd have a look at this poor chap,' he said, casting his eyes down and partially unwrapping the bundle in his arms.

I thought I'd become fairly hardened to the sight of battered and bruised animals, but this one was in a truly pitiful condition. I could just about make out that it was a cat.

'Obviously been run over by something big, probably a lorry or a tractor. Whoever ran him over left him on the roadside.

Lucky someone happened to be passing in his car and spotted him,' he continued.

The impact must have been horrific. Christopher told me both the cat's front legs were broken and his head was crushed. Such was the force, it had knocked one of his eyes clean out of the socket.

Given the damage the cat had suffered, the driver who found him had at first assumed he was dead, but to his surprise – and distress – he had seen that he was still alive. The cat had carried on breathing unevenly all the way to Christopher's surgery. Christopher had taken one look at the poor, crumpled creature and had decided he would have to be put to sleep immediately. But the moment the cat had been placed on the table he had amazed everyone in the room by suddenly opening his remaining eye, looking up at the concerned faces and purring gently.

'Rex, it was as if he'd just woken up after a light afternoon nap,' said Christopher. 'Talk about nine lives. This one must have ninety.'

He'd immediately dropped the idea of putting the cat down. Instead, with great skill and care, he'd set his two broken legs, removed his many broken teeth, dressed the empty eye socket and placed the patient under the warm glow of an infrared lamp in his intensive-care unit. The cat had remained there for almost a fortnight.

'He's on the road to recovery now, I think,' he said, giving the cat a reassuring stroke.

I still wasn't entirely sure why Christopher had come over to show me the cat. I could see the cat's legs were still in plaster casts and his eye was covered in a large gauze patch. He was doing a sterling job in caring for the poor creature, so why did he want me to look at him? For a moment there was an awkward silence.

'So how can I help?' I asked eventually.

'Oh, sorry, I thought you and Julie could take over his recuperation. We haven't got any space to keep him at the surgery,' he replied.

He obviously registered the surprised look that must have flashed across my face.

'Sorry, Rex, I couldn't think where else to bring him,' he said.

My wife, Julie, and I had moved to our cottage, the Rosery, in the small village of Bolingey, three-quarters of a mile or so from the north Cornwall coast, a year earlier, in 1960. We'd arrived with our two-year-old son, Glen, and had since welcomed a second boy, Alan, into the world. Our family had been completed by some pigeons, a terrier called Tammy, a cat called Sabi, three Muscovy ducks and a steady procession of part-time guests like One Eye.

We'd become a magnet for people such as Christopher for a couple of reasons. Firstly, in a county still dominated by farming and in particular the care of cattle, sheep and pigs, at that time there were very few vets who specialised in non-agricultural animals. Furthermore, the number of animal shelters devoted to cats and dogs, birds and other small animals in the vast swathe of countryside that ran between Plymouth and Land's End could be counted on the fingers of one hand. So as someone who'd always been interested in animals, and birds especially, I'd acquired something of a reputation for being willing to lend an occasional helping hand, providing shelter for birds with broken wings, stray dogs, cats and other creatures. Many of the animals we took in were referred to us by local vets with whom I had struck up a friendship. Others were delivered by people who had simply got to hear about us by word of mouth. Since moving to the Rosery, we'd provided a temporary home to scores of different species. Once we'd nursed them back to health, we'd either release them into the wild or find them a new home.

This latest arrival was a worry, however, and not because it was in such a bad way physically. The sad truth was, the cat population was spiralling out of control in our corner of the country. Spaying and neutering were not carried out on a regular basis, so most female cats produced kittens at least twice a year. This, coupled with the fact that Cornwall was also home to a large population of feral cats, meant that there were hundreds, if not thousands, of displaced cats roaming around.

I had found good homes for a fair few of them, but it felt like I was fighting a losing battle. For all these reasons, I had severe doubts this cat would ever find a home. I knew it wasn't easy to persuade people to take on even the most beautiful of adult cats, let alone a badly broken, one-eyed victim of a road accident.

I was not going to turn him away, though. By now our small garden had been fitted out with a series of pens with runs that had been converted into a cattery, as well as a couple of aviaries for wild-bird casualties. I knew there was space for the newcomer in the cattery, plaster casts and all. I placed him carefully in a comfortable corner.

'There you go, One Eye,' I said. 'See how you like it here.'

As a long-haired cat, One Eye needed daily grooming. The moment I took a brush to him a couple of days later, I discovered he was riddled with fleas. In fact he had more fleas than I'd seen on any cat. Luckily, he simply loved being combed and brushed. Each time I produced a brush he rolled on to his back in sheer bliss, happily submitting to the flea powder being rubbed into his fur. Within days he was putting on weight, and within a few weeks his tabby coat had started to take on a healthy sheen. When the day arrived for the removal of the plaster casts, it was clear that the operation had been a success.

His legs had mended perfectly. He was soon standing up confidently and walking tentatively around the cattery.

His future remained unclear, however. Yes, apart from several broken teeth and an empty eye socket, One Eye was a normal, healthy young cat, but who on earth was going to give an unconventional-looking creature like this a home?

I've taken on too much this time. I'll never get rid of this one, I fretted to myself.

Julie and I had moved to the Rosery from our previous home in a large caravan, set in a rather lovely hillside garden on the other side of the valley. We had started living in the caravan in 1958. It had been cosy, but it had only taken us a couple of years to outgrow it. With a baby and a small collection of animals installed there, it had always been a little cramped. When Julie fell pregnant for a second time, it was clear we would have to move somewhere more spacious, so we'd bought the Rosery, a 200-year-old stone cottage with two bedrooms, a small sitting room, a living room and kitchen. It also had the most wonderful outside loo, with a Victorian pan patterned with sprays of flowers.

When the locals had heard I was considering buying the Rosery, one or two of them had advised me against it. It had certainly needed a lot of work to be brought up to date, but we had decided to take on the challenge, and after a great deal of hard work it was taking shape.

First off, we had undertaken the major things that needed doing inside the house. We had renewed the old, cracked concrete floors, put in an Aga to replace the Cornish range, installed an indoor toilet and bathroom, and treated the wooden floors upstairs against the ravages of woodworm. Most importantly of all, we had tackled the damp that had afflicted the house during our early days there. Like many traditional Cornish cottages, the Rosery was built with its back wall set right into the countryside – in this case, a bank of soil and rock, higher than the cottage roof. This had made it difficult to even walk round the cottage, but also, because the soil had been allowed to build up over the years, it had affected the interior wall so that it was always damp. This had left the living room with a musty, damp smell that was unpleasant, not to mention extremely unhealthy.

We had discovered just how bad a problem the damp was when we had eventually removed the metre-high wooden panelling that covered the lower part of the back wall in the living room. Behind it was a huge expanse of dry rot. It was black and evil-looking, with tendrils that stretched upwards and vanished into the room above. We had later found that the fungi had extended right into the cottage roof, creeping up behind layers of whitewash.

It had taken us an age to rip out the panels, scrape the walls clear and eventually dig out the fungi and the soil in which it had flourished. The difference it made to the atmosphere inside the house, however, had been well worth the effort.

When our second son, Alan, was born in the bedroom here, two years after his brother, his first lungfuls of air were filled not with the stale smell of damp but the sweet whiff of honeysuckle wafting in from the garden.

The fact that such smells were now blowing in was down to yet more hard work. The garden had been in an equally ramshackle state as the cottage. It did, however, have the distinct advantage of facing south, so it was protected from the east and north winds. Julie and I had capitalised on this and planted a variety of flowers and shrubs, many of which soon began to bloom spectacularly.

On the cottage wall, a red-flowered cydonia had already

provided us with enough quinces for Julie to have produced her first batch of jam. There was also yellow winter jasmine, coronilla and that most beautiful of climbing roses, mermaid. Between them they had turned our little haven into a riot of colour. Entwined among them all was a swathe of evergreen honeysuckle, which filled the air with its intoxicating scent.

One part of the garden had remained deliberately untouched through all these changes, however. The ancient elder tree that stood, gnarled and twisted, next to the old outside toilet was a reminder of Cornwall's dark, superstitious past. Hundreds of years ago, when the cottage was built, the tree was believed to have magical powers; indeed, it was thought every home needed an elder so as to fend off witches. It was, we knew, a piece of silly folklore, but we weren't going to take the risk.

The most recent additions to the garden were the array of cages and sheds we'd erected to cope with the animals that were coming our way. In the space of our first year we'd had animals delivered not just from the public but from pet shops and bird gardens, even a zoo. Just about every corner of the garden was now occupied by some kind of pen or cage.

The garden had a good-sized wooden shed that had apparently once served as a schoolroom for three sisters and their private tutor. The shed had two rooms and I'd converted the smaller of these into a bird room, complete with an outside aviary. The range of birds that had already passed through was wide, from tiny lavender finches to crowned pigeons, a peafowl and a macaw.

The other enclosures were improvised affairs. If I ever saw an item of discarded furniture I wasted no time in requisitioning it. A three-drawer chest of drawers had, for instance, been converted into cages suitable for rabbits, guinea pigs and ferrets. Even the narrow space between the back of the cottage and the earth-and-stone wall had been utilised. I used this sheltered corner to rear young gulls. A pair I'd placed there when they'd arrived lost and exhausted had prospered.

'Have you seen One Eye today?' Julie asked matter-of-factly, returning from the cattery one morning. 'There's no sign of him anywhere.'

He had been with us for four weeks now, and as his condition had improved, One Eye had been given the freedom to roam around. He was fond of the garden and would lie on the boundary wall in the sunshine, his paws in the air so as to let the warmth soak into his fur, smiling at everyone who passed by the cottage and answering with his loud purr whenever he was spoken to.

Knowing this, the wall was one of the first places I looked this morning, but there was no sign of him. As I did my customary tour of the cattery and the other outbuildings, there was no evidence of him being there either.

In truth, I wasn't unduly concerned. I assumed he was off on a hunting expedition. There were plenty of rich pickings in the countryside at this time of year. He was probably enjoying himself chasing birds or perhaps a rabbit. When he didn't return that night, I didn't give it too much thought. There were more than enough places to take shelter for the night in the surrounding fields and hedgerows. And One Eye had already proved that he was more than capable of looking after himself. In a case like this all we could do was wait.

It was almost a week later that I heard via a friend that a long-haired tabby cat had been seen courting the lady cats at a farm a mile or so away.

'That can only be One Eye,' I said to Julie. 'I'd better head over there.'

My concern now was that he might be sowing his seed far

and wide. In the immediate aftermath of his arrival at the Rosery, I'd not thought it a priority to have One Eye neutered. He'd been in such a parlous state, I didn't think he would ever have the energy or the inclination to chase a female cat again. Even when he'd started to recover, it had never really crossed my mind to take him to the vet's for the snip. Clearly I'd underestimated him. He wasn't just a resilient cat, he was a spirited one too.

Admirable as One Eye's behaviour was in some respects, I knew that no farmer was going to appreciate having a promiscuous feline roaming his farm when his cats were in season. My oversight now looked like irresponsibility. I drove to the farm where he had been spotted, slightly fearful of what I might discover.

To my disappointment, One Eye was nowhere to be found. The farmer suspected he had been up to no good, but clearly time alone would tell if this was the case. I asked him to keep me informed. In the days that followed, however, it was other local folk who called, each of them reporting sightings of our distinctive guest. Our one-eyed Romeo was seemingly enjoying himself on a lady-killing spree.

'How am I ever going to lecture anyone on their responsibilities as cat owners?' I groaned to Julie over a cup of tea in the kitchen. 'I've let loose the randiest cat in all of Cornwall.'

I was placing some newly arrived kittens in a pen one morning a few days later when the Lothario finally reappeared. It was the familiar purr that alerted me to his presence. I looked up and there he was, back at his favourite spot, relaxing in the sun on the boundary wall, looking fat and contented, as well he might do.

'Well, fancy seeing you.' I smiled, inwardly delighted to have him back.

One Eye replied with a deep rumble of purrs and much

flailing of paws. He'd clearly had a great time and was itching to tell me about it.

'We'd better get him neutered in case he does it again,' Julie said over supper that night.

'I'll get down to the vet next week,' I agreed.

Next morning, however, I walked out into the yard to see One Eye in hot pursuit of another potential female conquest. As they ran out on to the road, the pair of them missed the wheels of a passing milk lorry by, well, a whisker.

'Never put off until tomorrow what you can do today,' I said to One Eye, as I scooped him up, slipped him into a cat basket and headed off to the vet's. His days as the Casanova of Cornish cats were soon brought to an end.

Caring for the assorted animals we had accumulated at the Rosery could easily have been a full-time job. Unfortunately, I already had one of those, working as the local postman. Early each morning I'd do a quick tour of the animal sheds in the garden, then hop on my bicycle to make the short ride to the sorting office in the town of Perranporth, where I'd start work at a quarter past six.

To me, it was a dream job. My previous employment had been at the local knitting mill, which had kept me indoors for long hours. To be free to travel the Cornish countryside each day was, to me at least, a privilege. There was even something exhilarating about the morning bike ride to work. My journey took me down a valley along a narrow road that wound its way through marshes towards the sea. Tasting the first salty tang of the sea breeze was always invigorating, even on the coldest morning, and as I meandered through the countryside, each season brought something new to appreciate and wonder at. In spring it was the buds on the sallows and the song of the newly arrived warblers. The summer mornings brought the warm coconut smell of the flowering gorse filtering through the valley as the sun rose and the air would be filled with swallows and martins, hawking early flying insects over the reeds. In autumn it was the mists that wreathed the marshes, lending the air a damp, earthy smell. When winter arrived, it was the sheer brute force of the northerly gales that blew in from the sea and could be so strong I had to dismount the bike and push into them. They never spoiled the journey much.

As a postman in the 1960s, I also felt I was playing an important role in the local community. It wasn't just the sociable side of the job, although, within the more isolated areas, the friendly face I provided was very important to some. It was the fact that the postman, back then at least, was an important link with the outside world, someone who could help people out in times of need. Barely a day went by when I didn't run a shopping errand or collect a prescription for someone on my round, and in return barely a day went by when I wasn't invited into someone's house for a cup of tea.

The job was made all the more enjoyable by the colourful collection of individuals who worked with me at the sorting office, which was made up of the postmaster, Doug, four full-timers and one part-time postman. The part-timer was a lay Methodist preacher, a short man with a great sense of humour, which he needed to put up with some of the crude language that flew around the sorting office at times. He was a wonderfully calm and kind person who never had a bad word to say about anyone. If he ever got exasperated, the worst he could manage was to call them a 'bufflehead'. Of the three full-timers, two used to be military men. One was an ex-sergeant major, who when he wasn't at the post office was organising the local surf rescue operation. The other, the office's great character, was an ex-RAF flight sergeant called Ray. Ray had lost an arm when a helicopter had crashed at an air show, and wore a flexible metal hook at the end of his replacement limb. The handicap didn't slow him down in the sorting office, however. He could sort the day's supply of several hundred letters as fast, if not faster, than the rest of us. Ray's accident had done nothing to dampen his sense of humour either. In fact it had given him an additional prop for his jokes.

Every now and again we'd pop into the local pub for a drink in the evening. On one occasion we entered the bar to discover a very large Great Dane in residence. Ray had his back to the bar and was talking to the dog when a new barmaid appeared from the back of the pub, where she'd been fetching in some stock.

Seeing Ray with the dog, she reassured him, 'Oh, don't worry about the dog, sir, he won't hurt you.'

As it was the end of the working day, Ray had taken off his hook. He turned to the barmaid and held up his sleeve, then let the stump of his prosthetic arm poke through. 'Don't worry, you say,' he said, his face fixed in a stone-cold expression. 'Then what about this?'

The barmaid promptly fainted.

While I enjoyed working as a postman, it didn't pay enough to keep a young family fed and clothed, so I supplemented my income with extra jobs in the community. By day I did a little gardening work for people in the area, but far more enjoyable for me was the dog-clipping service I ran in the evenings and at weekends. Locals would leave their dogs with me for grooming and clipping. The diversity of breeds, the styles of cutting required and, of course, the temperaments on display made it an interesting and at times eventful job. In fact, there was hardly ever a dull moment.

Today, of course, poodle parlours strap dogs to special stands where they can be groomed and clipped efficiently. No such contraptions existed then, and even if they did I wouldn't have been able to afford one. Instead I simply stood the dog on a table, then clipped or combed away, talking to the dog as I did so. The dog's reward for behaving well was a run in the field afterwards while we waited for the owner to return. It must have worked well because as a rule most of my canine clients were well behaved and came back to me on a regular basis.

Things didn't always go according to plan, of course.

On one occasion I had bathed, groomed and clipped a lovely white poodle bitch. She jumped down from my table gleaming. The moment she was let loose in the field, however, she let out a loud yelp and dived straight into a large, moist cowpat. She then proceeded to roll around in it until her entire coat had turned a brownish-green. In a panic, I retrieved her and put her back into the bath. I managed to remove most of the mess, but she went home smelling less fragrant than a well-bred poodle should.

I also saw the best and worst of owners. One Pekinese was brought to us to be rehomed by a woman who could no longer cope with the expense of looking after him. When I took over caring for him, I discovered that the poor little dog's coat was so heavy and matted that no amount of combing would return it to its natural healthy state, so instead I got out the clippers and took the coat right off. The final cut was within an inch or two of the dog's skin.

By the time I was finished I had a pile of hair higher than the Peke himself. I also had a rather shocked-looking little dog. When I placed him on the floor shorn of his old coat, the poor chap couldn't even get his balance and fell over several times before finding his equilibrium. Being a Peke, however, he quickly regained his dignity and humour, and was soon running around unhampered by matted hair for the first time in many months.

At the other end of the scale, some dog owners were so protective they would try to insist on staying with their pets while I worked. From the very beginning, though, this was something I had to be firm about. Dogs, I knew well, were just like children in this respect: they tended to play up when their parents were around and be much better behaved when alone with a stranger.

A prime example of this was a long-haired German shepherd who used to arrive with his owner and would snap and snarl at everyone. The minute his owner left, however, his whole manner changed and he would allow himself to be combed without even a growl. Of course, the second his owner came back, he returned to his aggressive self.

I understood what lay at the root of this. The owner's worry about the dog's temperament exacerbated the situation, creating a vicious circle. The more he fretted, the more his anxiety transmitted to the dog, who felt he had to protect the owner from whatever was worrying him.

I was being paid to clip and trim dogs, not counsel their owners. It wasn't easy, but I kept my opinions to myself. I needed the money.

I emerged from the house early one morning to see a familiar pair of faces approaching the garden gate. Mr and Mrs Stone were a newly retired couple who had just moved into the village. We often saw them walking past on their daily stroll round the village.

'Good morning, Mr Harper,' said Mr Stone. 'We were wondering whether you might have a cat that would make us a good companion.'

As word of our miniature sanctuary spread, we were beginning to get occasional visits of this kind.

I was more than happy to let them see what we had to offer

and ushered them to the cattery. Several kittens were available, and as usual I saw the visitors wrestling with the decision. So many things can influence a person's choice – colour, personality, size, all these things come into the equation. In this particular case, however, things were made much simpler by the sudden and unexpected arrival of One Eye.

I don't know how he knew Mr and Mrs Stone had come to visit, but he wasted no time in weaving his way round the couple's legs, brushing against their ankles and purring like a sewing machine.

'We know this chap well.' Mrs Stone smiled. 'He's always on your wall when we pass by on our walks. We've had many a chat with you, haven't we, mister?'

Mr Stone was smiling at him too. 'Tell me, Mr Harper,' he said. 'Whatever happened to his eye?'

As I told the story of how One Eye had come to us, I saw both their faces crumpling.

Mrs Stone was close to tears and was soon crouching down to stroke him. 'You poor thing,' she said.

One Eye turned up the volume on his purr and smiled craftily. By the end of the morning Mr and Mrs Stone had gone home, popped to the nearest pet shop, bought a cat cage and returned.

To my amazement – and, I must admit, relief – One Eye had finally found a permanent home, and a good one at that. I wasn't so sentimental as to think every abandoned or damaged creature that came our way was going to find a home in this way, but it did make me realise that I shouldn't be so quick to write off animals. Their resilience, and guile, was not to be underestimated.

Soon afterwards I happened to be passing the Stones' cottage and thought I'd check on One Eye's progress. I found Mrs Stone sitting by the fire with One Eye draped across her feet.

'Does he ever wander these days?' I asked her.

'What, and chance missing a meal?' She grinned. 'Oh, no, there's no fear of that.'

One Eye looked up at me, purring that all too familiar purr, the sound that had saved his life. As he did so, I swear he closed his one good eye for a second as if to wink at me.

CHAPTER TWO

First Loves

Looking back, I suppose it's easy to see why my love of animals took root so early in my life. As an only child, insects and birds, dogs and rabbits provided me with the companionship that was too often missing at home. And as my youth unfolded, nature's abundant life provided a constancy that, tragically, the people close to me could not.

I was born in the beautiful city of Bath in 1935. My father had died of diabetes four months before I was born, leaving my mother to raise me. She shared that job with her mother, my grandmother, whose little bungalow on the outskirts of the city was my boyhood home. My first memories are of the garden there. It was filled with flowers: roses, Michaelmas daisies and, in the spring, large bushes of heavily scented lilac, red hawthorn and magnolia. As a small boy, the garden seemed enormous and full of potential, particularly when I discovered that the stones in the rock garden hid a variety of creepy crawlies, which could be caught, imprisoned in a jam jar and observed at my leisure. The assortment of earwigs, woodlice and centipedes I amassed in my grandmother's garden became my first pets. They were quickly joined by grasshoppers and butterflies, with the odd spider and unusual-looking snail thrown in for good measure.

My mother, it has to be said, wasn't too enamoured of my collection. Every now and again a member of my microscopic menagerie would escape from its jar and take up residence in a cupboard or wardrobe, much to her horror. My grandmother, on the other hand, was hugely encouraging. She was a great animal lover and would read natural-history books to me, which I greatly enjoyed, asking endless questions.

As I sat on my grandmother's knee, the one subject I didn't ask many questions about was my father. As a result I know very little about him. The main thing I gleaned was that he had worked in a jeweller's in Bath. But my grandmother also told me that he had had a great love of the countryside. Deep down, I wonder whether knowing this might somehow have encouraged me in my love of the natural world. Who can say?

I was the only child of pre-school age growing up in the cul-de-sac where my grandmother lived. So, around 1940, when the time came to go to school, I found it hard to adjust to other children, particularly given that very few of them shared my interest in animals and natural history in general. This seemed very strange to me, but it did nothing to dampen my enthusiasm for nature; in fact it probably did the complete opposite.

It was around the time I started school that I acquired my

first real pet, a male Dutch rabbit called Whiskers. He was given to me by a local policeman who I suspect was rather smitten with my mother. Our garden shed was quickly fitted with a wire-framed door and became Whiskers's hutch. He lived there, a happy – if perhaps a little lonesome – rabbit, for most of my childhood.

It was Whiskers who brought me closer to the only other child who lived on our street. Heather was six years older than me and seemed, to me at least, very mature. By this time the Second World War was well under way, and as part of a scheme to encourage people to produce more food at home, Heather had started keeping a number of rabbits. She shared my passion for nature and proved to be a mine of useful information. In return for snippets of advice, I helped her clean out her rabbits' cages. We became firm friends. In a very real sense, she became the sister I never had.

As the war intensified, the realities of the conflict began to hit closer to home. Every night the wail of air-raid sirens and the roar of planes filled the skies, as did the red glow on the horizon to the west, the telltale sign that the port of Bristol was once more burning under a constant barrage of incendiary bombs. Bath was hit too, suffering many bombing raids. Whole streets of houses were razed to the ground, and church spires stood forlornly alongside the shattered remains of their chancels.

The bomb sites were declared 'out of bounds', especially to children, but they became irresistible, to me at least, mainly because they were filled with nature. Great banks of the 'bomb-site flower' rose-bay willow herb and buddleia seedlings took root among the nooks and crannies of the rubble, and in a matter of a few months the stark ruins had become a wild garden attracting all manner of insects and birds. Inside the shell-like remains of large buildings, there were jackdaws, kestrels and owls. My personal favourites were the beautiful feral pigeons that flourished there. I spent many happy, if somewhat dangerous, hours climbing around the ruins, looking for their nests and noting their behaviour.

It wasn't long before I'd acquired my first collection of the birds. There was something wonderful about keeping them. They were relatively easy to tame, but of course what made pigeons such great pets was their ability to fly free, then return home to their lofts. Other boys got excited about sport or hanging around in gangs, but for me there was nothing to compare with the feeling I got from waiting for a pigeon to return home from a training flight. I would rattle its feed tin, then stare at the skies, waiting for a dark speck to appear. It never ceased to thrill me when the pigeon zoomed in, folded its wings and dived down on to the landing board, alighting with a swish of its wings. It would then hold its head high and strut and coo to its mates as if to say, 'Did you see that?'

At the age of eleven I moved on to secondary school, but it did little to improve my academic abilities. I enjoyed art, geography and English, but to my great frustration there was no mention of the natural world or biology. Sport seemed the school's overwhelming priority, but I couldn't work up any enthusiasm for kicking a ball around or holding a cricket bat, so games lessons became a bore. Instead I devoted more and more time to my collection of animals, which, as well as homing pigeons, had now grown to include white mice, guinea pigs and bantams. Most of all, I devoted myself to the animal that had quickly become my closest companion in the world, my first dog, Sally.

I had Heather to thank for bringing her into my life. By now in her late teens, Heather had left school and had progressed from working at a local boarding kennels to starting a small kennel of her own, breeding a variety of spaniels. I would help out there after school and in the holidays. When Heather decided to concentrate on breeding just cocker spaniels, Sally, a lovely Sussex spaniel bitch, became surplus to requirements. I could barely believe it when Heather offered her to me. Sally was red and gold, a little heavier in build than a cocker spaniel with a longer body too. She was two years old when Heather gave her to me and had already produced one litter of seven pups.

She taught me much about the joys of dog ownership. From the outset she was the friendliest of dogs and the perfect companion. If I was happy, Sally shared my joy as we ran across the water meadows or paddled in the river. If I was moody or depressed, she would sit beside me, seemingly listening to my problems, content to quietly keep me company.

We had our share of adventures, none more exciting than when Sally decided to chase a moorhen across a river. She was a great swimmer, and one winter's day when the river Avon was in flood she spotted a moorhen on the far bank. Before I realised what was happening, Sally was swimming her way across the wide, turbulent expanse of river, fighting the strong current with some difficulty here and there. My heart was in my mouth at times. Needless to say, the moorhen had long gone by the time Sally arrived on the other side of the river. Undeterred, she plunged straight back in and headed towards me. The return trip was even more of a strain on my nerves than the outward leg. Sally was obviously tired and made heavy weather of the swim, often allowing herself to be carried downstream. At times she seemed to vanish amid the brown swirling water and I had real doubts that she'd make it. But eventually she did, collapsing on the bank at my feet, smiling up at me, with her tail as always happily wagging.

With a dog to share my life, school became even less of an

interest to me. During sports periods, I began slipping away unnoticed and sneaking back home, where a quiet whistle would summon Sally to join me. We would head off to the countryside, and Sally would sit patiently by my side as I went fishing for newts and sticklebacks. At other times we would walk to Kelston Round Hill, an ancient burial mound. The place was alive with wildlife, from foxes and brown hares to buzzards, which were very rare in those days. I spent many an hour lying in the long grass there, looking down on the crater of Bath, or Bristol away to the west.

I only got caught playing truant once and received a well-deserved caning for it. It should have stopped me trying to escape, but it didn't. All it did was make me more careful.

Looking back to those long-ago days, I get the odd pang of guilt at not having applied myself more to my school-work. But it doesn't last long. I know that the self-taught knowledge I gained from my illicit expeditions has served me well.

I didn't realise it at the time, but the most significant moment of my young life came two years after the end of the war, in 1947, when I was twelve or so. As we were cleaning out the cages at Heather's kennels one evening, she broke the news that she and her family were moving to Cornwall.

They were taking over a smallholding at Wheal Francis, a hamlet near the north-coast village of Perranporth. It was a hammer blow to me, not just because I knew I'd miss the routine of helping out at the kennels. To be honest, I didn't have many close friends. She was the only young person with whom I shared a genuine rapport.

It was a sad day when we waved Heather and her family goodbye and watched the removals lorry bumping its way down the road.

With Heather gone, I was slightly lost for a while, but then I managed to find myself another animal-related job, this time working at a pet shop in Bath. I worked there on weekends and in the school holidays. On the rare weekends I had off, I used the money I saved from skipping school dinners to catch a bus to Bristol and the city's Natural History Museum and, of course, its zoo. I spent many long hours there, studying every living thing I saw.

The zoo taught me a great deal, but so did the pet shop. No animal taught me as much, or provided me with as much fun, as a female pig-tailed macaque monkey called Ginny. Ginny was a particularly headstrong creature. One day she escaped from her cage at the rear of the shop, walked calmly out of the shop door and, after somehow managing to negotiate the busy main road, climbed high into the topmost branches of an acacia tree, where she remained for four days, steadfastly refusing to be tempted down with offers of her favourite food. In the end the fire brigade came to the rescue, resulting in much publicity for both themselves and the pet shop.

Ginny had a tender side to her as well and was very maternal. She would 'mother' kittens or even hamsters if she could get hold of them, never hurting them. Indeed her affection for her brood was so deep it could be difficult to get her to hand them over when it was time for her to return to her cage.

I formed a deep bond with her. One day I was getting ready to leave the shop on my bike when Ginny suddenly appeared and jumped on the handlebars. She sat there clearly enjoying herself as I cycled around for a moment or two. The next day I decided to slip a collar round her waist, tethered her lead to the crossbar of the bike and headed off into the countryside with her and Sally. The three of us had a whale of a time together.

Eventually Ginny proved too much of a handful for everyone at the pet shop. We also felt she needed company, so she was presented to Bristol Zoo, where she joined a group of macaques and produced a baby of her own.

By the time I was fifteen I was ready to leave school. I did so without the benefit of any qualifications, but also with no regrets, and started to look for a full-time job. During my more fanciful moments at school I had dreamed of being a vet at a zoo or a plant hunter. I had visions of travelling to far-flung corners of the world, risking my life in war zones to get a sample of a rare flower or plant. The reality was that I left school singularly unqualified for either role. Indeed it was hard to imagine what I was cut out for.

Working at a zoo wasn't entirely out of the question, however. Somehow I obtained an interview with the curator of Bristol Zoo, who to my delight was persuaded I might make a good trainee keeper. The elation I felt at being offered a job was short-lived. When I looked at the financial side of things, the rather paltry weekly wage I'd get only just covered my bus fares to Bristol from Bath and back. It was a non-starter. I would have to come up with another plan.

Before I could do so, however, my mother returned from a stay with Heather and her parents in Cornwall. She had been through a difficult period. My grandmother had died and she had decided, after many years doing voluntary work for charities, that it was time for a change in her life. Arriving back from Cornwall, she announced that she had decided what that change should be. She told me that she had fallen in love with the area in which Heather's family now lived. Not only that, she had bought a house there.

The news came as something of a bombshell. I loved Bath and the surrounding countryside. But when I heard that I had been invited to stay at Heather's smallholding and that there was a very good chance of a job at her kennels, I began to open my mind to the idea.

As I headed off on my first trip to Cornwall, nothing could have prepared me for the impact that the county would have on me. Crossing the Tamar in the train for the first time, I experienced a feeling of belonging that has stayed with me almost all my life. By the time I reached Truro on that first journey I was captivated by the Cornish countryside, and the sight of the towering and beautiful cathedral as the train pulled into the station was the clincher: I wanted to live there too.

The hamlet Heather and her family had moved to only added to the county's instant appeal. Set in a wooded valley abundant with wildlife, Wheal Francis was my idea of heaven. The kennels were thriving, and Heather and her parents reassured me there was a job waiting for me when I moved down.

My mother had found a home near Wheal Francis, in the picturesque village of Bolingey. She'd had an offer accepted on a cottage and back home had also found a buyer for our bungalow. I set off back for Bath knowing that I would soon be returning to the south-west and a new life in Cornwall.

And so it was that one morning, in September 1950, I climbed into the back of a friend's van with Sally, another dog, a canary, six pigeons and eight hens. It was a bumpy but memorable journey. By the time we reached Perranporth in mid-afternoon, several of the chickens had laid eggs.

My mother had sent me on ahead, so I arrived in Bolingey on my own. I busied myself setting up temporary pens for the hens and pigeons and putting up a camp bed for myself. I had set off with a healthy supply of sandwiches and was just about to sit down on an orange box to tuck into my supper when there was a knock on the door. The rather plump lady I found on the doorstep introduced herself as Mrs Luscombe, our next-door neighbour. She had a small plate in her hand, upon which was sitting a large half-moon-shaped golden pasty.

'Hope you don't mind me calling, but me and my husband, Fred, saw you here on your own and popped a pasty in the oven for you,' she said.

It was my first taste of Cornish hospitality, but far from my last.

Strangers moving to the south-west of England from elsewhere in the UK, or 'up country' as the locals put it, were something of a rarity in the 1950s. Cornwall was a poor and isolated corner of the country. But the people of Bolingey made us welcome from the beginning.

The village was little more than a few cottages, several of which were thatched. There was a large chapel, a pub, a village shop, a community centre run by the charity Toc H and a general store. There was also a 'greengrocer's', although in reality it was someone's living room laid out with boxes of fresh fruit and vegetables.

Like any village, Bolingey had more than its share of characters. The corn mill was run by a man called Mr Hodge, who, to my fifteen-year-old eyes, looked to be about ten times my age. Despite his advancing years and his short, thin build, he moved the heavy sacks of grain around with amazing, almost balletic ease, sending clouds of dust into the air and attracting flocks of sparrows to pick at the spilled corn on the mill floor. Then there was Mrs Widdicombe, the owner of the village shop and post office. When it came to goings-on in Bolingey, she was the fount of all knowledge – and gossip. Despite her rather forbidding appearance, she was a kindly soul. Food rationing was still a part of life then. When I called in for my weekly sweet ration, she would give me the value of my coupons, then slip a couple of extra humbugs into my bag with a conspiratorial wink and a whispered, 'There you are, my boy.'

But the character who made by far the biggest impact on me was Howard, a giant of a man who earned his living trapping rabbits. In the early 1950s rabbits provided our part of Cornwall with one of its few sources of steady income. Each day hundreds of rabbits would be loaded on to the trains at Truro Station, destined for the kitchens and food stores 'up country'. The methods employed to maintain the daily supply of rabbit meat weren't pleasant. Trappers used snares, which caught the rabbits in a wire noose round the neck, or gin traps – now thankfully illegal – which were buried under the soil and captured victims by the leg, usually severing the bone and causing much suffering.

I got to know Howard fairly soon after arriving in Bolingey. Once I'd convinced him I wasn't 'another one of those bloody emits from up country', he let me accompany him on his morning rounds, touring the woods and sand dunes for rabbits captured overnight. He was the most knowledgeable of countrymen and taught me a huge amount.

I can't deny that I found his business distasteful. The suffering the rabbits endured was hideous. The best I could do as I joined Howard on his morning rounds was to ensure any rabbits I found caught in a trap were put out of their misery as quickly as possible. I dispatched them with a quick blow to the head, then tied them to the pile of carcasses, which would grow until it weighed what felt like a ton by the end of the morning.

Trapping rabbits was, of course, an imprecise science and other animals would become ensnared in Howard's traps. On many occasions I would release a cat and it would hobble off home, probably condemned to a life limping. Every now and again I found a badger caught in a gin trap. Invariably the scene was one of complete carnage. Given the strength of their bones, they were rarely badly injured by the traps. An ensnared badger would, however, be extremely annoyed and agitated by being held captive and would dig up and generally destroy the surrounding area as it tried in vain to escape. Howard taught me how to release a badger from a trap, a tricky procedure, given that they have sharp teeth and are not afraid to use them. It was a skill that was to come in extremely useful later in life.

Howard also caught rabbits by another means, lamping. This involved going out in the late evening armed with a flashlight and his dog, an impressive lurcher called Jack. Rabbits tend to emerge from their burrows at dusk to feed in the fields. When Howard spotted a group, he would turn his spotlight on them, making them freeze – rather like the old expression – in the headlights. In the few moments that the rabbits were immobilised, Jack would be dispatched to pick one up in his teeth. In what seemed a flash, the dog would grab a rabbit and return to his master holding the animal alive in his teeth. Once the rabbit was handed over, Jack would stand there trembling with excitement at the prospect of being released again.

My childhood city, Bath, had been rich in wildlife, but Bolingey was home to an even more fascinating diversity of animals. The village was built on the hillsides either side of a wide valley, through which a fast-moving stream wound its way to the sea through an expanse of marshes and reed-beds. Every winter the stream would flood, leaving the main road that ran along the valley under water. The few cottages built at the bottom of the valley were invariably flooded too. On more than one occasion I saw people walking up and down the valley knee-deep in water.

For someone as fascinated with wildlife as I was, this watery landscape was a paradise on earth, an environment teeming with animals, and birds in particular. The marshes attracted a huge variety of birdlife. During the summer they were filled with warblers, nesting amid the reeds. I spent hours watching sedge warblers shooting up over the reed-beds, turning on impressive displays of flying, or listening out for the distinctive trill of the reed warbler, hidden away in the thick overgrowth. Water rails also bred in the marshes and I got occasional glimpses of these shy birds, often followed by their brood of black chicks. Around the fringes of the marsh, there were also cirl buntings, a species, sadly now vanished, that looked rather like a yellowhammer. As if this birdlife wasn't impressive enough, the village and its wooded valley were filled with other winged wonders, from woodlarks and skylarks to swallows, swifts and martins. There were even sightings of the ghostly barn owl, a few of which nested in the large chimneys of Bolingey's thatched cottages.

As I approached my seventeenth birthday, I had established a new life for myself. My mother and I were happily settled in Bolingey. I was working at the kennels as much as I could with Heather, and I had made a couple of other close friends. One, in particular, a fourteen-year-old boy named David, was a keen birdwatcher too. We spent many a weekend cycling to the cliffs and isolated beaches together, and visiting islands off the north Cornish coast, studying the myriad species that populated our corner of the country. Life seemed pretty much perfect. Or so I thought. I soon had my illusions shattered.

I hadn't been able to put my finger on it when I'd visited Heather in Cornwall the first time, but there was something slightly different about her. She seemed less happy than she had been in Bath. During my first months in Cornwall, the change in her became all the more obvious. The extremely active, strong and joyful girl I had known seemed to have been replaced by a lethargic, low-spirited person. It was most obvious when we were around the dogs. Since her earliest days breeding spaniels, Heather had been passionate about her kennels. Like me, she could have spent twenty-four hours a day feeding and grooming, walking and training dogs. Now she seemed uninterested and disconnected from them.

It was my mother who broke the news to me. One evening she sat me down and told me she had something important to tell me about Heather. In a grave voice and close to tears, she told me Heather had undergone a series of tests at the local hospital. They had revealed that she had cancer. She was being treated for it, but the diagnosis was not promising. She might not get better. She might die, my mother told me.

In the coming months, Heather's decline was dramatic and harrowing to witness. Within a year or so of my moving to Cornwall she had died, aged just twenty-three.

The loss was shattering. I was seventeen and had lost the person to whom I had felt closest during my young life. Heather had been the first young person who had shared my passion for nature. She had taught me a great deal, but she was also my closest friend, someone I could confide in.

Heather's death devastated her family. The kennels had to close, and the dogs were sold. I stayed on for a while, working for Heather's parents while they wound down the business. At times I found the loss too much to bear.

Around this time it struck me that I was now eligible to join the Forces, so I decided to try my luck with the RAF. I knew they had police dog handlers and, with my background, thought I might have a chance of training as one. It wasn't much of a plan, but it seemed to be a way of moving forward and putting some of the sadness of the last year behind me. So, in the autumn of 1952, I left Bolingey with hardly a backward glance. My mother had made a happy life for herself there and had many friends, but for me the place that had so smitten me when I had first moved there now held raw and painful memories. I had high hopes that my life with animals was going to continue. But it was going to happen somewhere far from Cornwall – or so I assumed.

CHAPTER THREE
The Bad Shepherd

I'd finished the day's deliveries and was just getting ready to head home from the sorting office when Doug, the postmaster, appeared and beckoned me into his office.

'Rex, can I have a quick word?' he said, a rather serious tone in his voice.

Another postman, Alan, was already in Doug's office. He was sitting down, drawing heavily on a cigarette and was looking agitated and a little distressed.

'Rex, is there any way you can swap rounds with Alan tomorrow morning?' Doug enquired. 'We thought you might be able to sort out this dog that's been causing him so much trouble.'

'Which dog's that?' I said. 'I didn't know you were having a problem.'

'He's a bloody great big German shepherd, Rex,' Alan said. 'He goes for me every single day. This morning he charged at me, jumped up and knocked me clean over. Really hurt my back in the fall,' he said, his voice trembling slightly, clearly still shaken by the experience. 'The worst thing about it is his owner,' Alan went on. 'He just stands there doing nothing. Thinks it's funny, I reckon.'

Dogs were, of course, the postman's traditional enemy. Like every post office in the country, I'm sure, we had our share of stories, most of which were serious, but one or two, I had to admit, had a funny side to them. The most amusing was that of Roger, a Scottish terrier who had started attacking Ray, another member of our quintet of postmen, on a daily basis. Every morning without fail he would wait for Ray to slip the post through the letterbox, then dash out and latch himself on to his leg, nipping away at his ankles as the poor fellow tried to escape.

Like so many owners, Roger's seemed to think the whole thing was a joke. Ray didn't, however, and in typical style he took rather drastic action. One morning, as Roger came tearing at him, Ray bent down and lifted up the yelping little dog by the scruff of the neck. He then dropped him unceremoniously over the low hedge that bordered the garden.

Unfortunately, Ray didn't realise that the stream that ran past the garden was in full flood. Roger was soon being swept downstream at a fair old rate of knots. Being a true terrier, Roger dealt with the situation. He swam to the bank, climbed out and shook himself off. Moments later he returned to the garden and headed towards the front door. Ray couldn't help smiling to himself at the sight of the soaking dog returning home, his tail very much between his legs. But Roger's owner wasn't quite so amused.

'What's happened to you?' she shrieked, as he rushed past her, intent on getting indoors.

'Don't worry, madam, he's just been for a swim,' Ray informed her with a wry smile.

Unsurprisingly, that was the last time Roger attacked Ray, or indeed any other postman. In fact he became really friendly with Ray, greeting him with a wag of his tail and a playful bark every morning from then on.

There was a big difference between a small terrier and a fully grown German shepherd, however. I could see that Alan had been badly upset by this dog. Clearly something needed to be done, for numerous reasons. Obviously no postman could carry on delivering to a home if he was being subjected to this kind of threat. We had to find a way for Alan to visit this address every day. The owner had to be sorted out too. Alan was right in this respect. Some owners did seem to take a genuine delight in seeing their pets terrorising tradesmen on a daily basis. This one had to be spoken to, in no uncertain terms. But, for reasons far deeper than Alan and Doug could have understood, I was most concerned for the dog. It needed help too, I suspected. Otherwise, if we were not careful, the consequences could be tragic.

'I'm happy to have a go. I'm sure we can sort it out,' I told Alan. 'Give me the address and I'll keep an eye out for the dog when I get there.'

'Thanks, Rex,' he said. 'But be careful – I think this one's a real handful.'

'Don't worry,' I replied. 'I'm sure I've seen worse.'

German shepherds had played an important part in my life. The first one I'd befriended was a bitch called Mitzi, who belonged to the owner of a shop I worked in as a teenager during the school holidays. Back then the breed still had a dark reputation, with strong associations with the war. Not many people kept them as domestic pets. But I'd been impressed by Mitzi's intelligence and loyalty, and had started taking her for long country walks.

Only once had Mitzi caused me a problem. One day during a thunderstorm we'd sought refuge in an isolated farmhouse. Unfortunately, the house contained a large tabby cat, which Mitzi had taken an instant dislike to. She had crashed around the kitchen, smashing crockery and leaving me feeling very embarrassed.

But it had been in the RAF that I had formed my deepest and most important friendship with a German shepherd. If it hadn't been for Ripper, my life might have turned out very differently indeed. I'd been seventeen and a half when I enlisted for the RAF. After the standard introductory spell of marching and square-bashing, I was posted to the RAF police school at Netheravon on Salisbury Plain. After six weeks' basic training as a service policeman, I moved on to the police-dog training school.

On the first day of the course I'd made the mistake of admitting to having some experience with Alsatians, as they were more commonly referred to then.

'Well, it seems we have an expert here,' the corporal had replied with a sadistic-looking grin. 'I think I've got just the dog for you.'

Each member of the course was allocated a dog with which he would have to work over the coming weeks. The aim of the exercise was to mould man and dog into a team. Later that morning I was introduced to Ripper, a sable-coloured dog with an intelligent face and bright yellow eyes.

Ripper had been put in a kennel attached to a running chain and had been set apart from the rest of the dogs at the school.

It didn't take me long to work out why. No sooner had I greeted him with a 'Hello, boy' than he was charging at me with his teeth bared and his hackles raised. If I hadn't run backwards across a boundary line that had been marked on the ground, he would almost certainly have mauled me. As it was, the long running chain brought him to a stop just inches from my face. He stood there for a moment, staring at me, his teeth clicking together like a pair of castanets.

'Didn't do a very good job with him, did you, my son,' the corporal shouted, with obvious glee. 'Tell you what, I'll give you a couple of days to see what you can do. If you ask me, he's a bloody menace and should be put down. But I'm happy to let you have a go at teaching him some manners.'

I discovered that Ripper had been badly mistreated as a young dog. By the time he arrived at the training school he was completely antisocial. He'd been put in isolation after attacking one of the WRAF kennel maids. He was deemed such a threat no one could go near him. Even his food was pushed towards him with the end of a long broom.

I felt he deserved a second chance, however, and set about trying to give it to him. I began by sitting down alongside him on the grass next to his kennel. If I stood up, he tried to attack at once, his yellow eyes full of fury and defiance. But if I kept calm, he remained at ease.

I stayed there with him all day, leaving only at the camp's mealtimes, and always returning from a different direction, so he got used to me arriving unexpectedly. By the evening, though, I noticed that Ripper was waiting for me. When I arrived after supper, he was standing there with his ears cocked, staring at the spot where he had last seen me. He still barked and reared up when I sat down, but the intensity of his anger had definitely dropped off. I'd tried talking to him earlier in the day but had found this had only increased his aggression. Instead I just greeted him with a gentle 'Hello, boy' and sat there. As I headed off for the night Ripper watched me every step of the way.

I carried on in the same vein the next morning. When I returned from a tea break midway through the morning, I was amazed to see that the telltale stiff, upright tail of the angry dog had been replaced by a slightly wagging one, a sure sign of a thawing of relations. I felt elated: here at last was a sign he was accepting me. By the end of the day Ripper had begun walking along the length of his run without going for me. When I lay down at the end of the afternoon, he moved as close as he could to me and adopted the same position.

Thinking back on it, today's health and safety regulations would never allow a seventeen-year-old lad to take such risks with a dangerous dog. The early 1950s were a very different time, however: if I wanted to take a chance, I could, provided I was ready for the consequences. That evening I decided to take the biggest risk yet. I crossed the boundary line beyond which I was within his range and approached the kennel. I had a rope lead and a check-chain. Carefully I slipped on the check-chain, unclipped the collar that was attached to his restraining chain and asked Ripper to walk with me. He was absolutely delighted. He jumped around with his tail waving from side to side like a windscreen wiper. We headed off across Salisbury Plain and walked for miles. By the time we returned it was dusk.

'Goodnight, boy,' I said, as I returned him to his kennel. I don't think I've ever felt so pleased with myself as I did back in the billet that night.

When we assembled for drill training the following morning, Ripper joined me in the ranks, standing still in line, ready for the corporal's inspection. I will never forget the look of amazement on the corporal's face.

'How the bloody hell did you manage that?' he said, walking towards us. Ripper took one look at him, then snarled and reared up. Fortunately, I had him on a short length of rope and was able to rein him in. 'Just keep him away from me, Harper,' the corporal said, looking flustered for once.

Ripper joined in the morning's drill with the rest of the dogs. He resented being asked to sit or lie down as required by the corporal and let me know in no uncertain terms. Whenever he went for my ankles or thighs I was grateful for the heavy denim trousers and thick webbing gaiters that were part of my uniform. I didn't give up, though. I knew he was making great strides.

By the end of the first week he was behaving pretty well on the parade ground, with only the occasional flash of the old temper. Off duty, however, he was the best friend a young man could wish for. Our walks across the plain got longer and longer. We had more fun too. Ripper particularly enjoyed play-fighting. I would chase him, bring him down with a kind of rugby tackle and playfully pin him to the ground. He would then chase me, leaping at my back and sending me flying. He would grab at my leg or arm, but never in such a way that he hurt me.

As our trust in one another grew, we became a close partnership. As part of the course we learned skills like agility and tracking and practised techniques like fending off criminal attacks and apprehending felons.

As close as we became, however, Ripper's attitude to others remained the same. Anyone approaching him was treated to bared teeth and a menacing series of barks. Ripper was particularly sensitive around mealtimes. The WRAF kennel maids still had to push his food bowl to him with the end of a broom.

When the course came to an end, we were gathered

together to hear our postings. Six of us were told that, along with our respective dogs, we were bound for the Far East. We had about six weeks to wait before heading out to Singapore. In the interim we would each be given part-time postings, in the case of Ripper and me, to Odiham in Hampshire. Our job was to guard the site of that year's Queen's Review, in which Her Majesty was treated to a display of flying by the RAF's finest. This involved patrolling the camp every night, something that I found extremely tiresome. It had an even more dramatic impact on Ripper. From the moment he arrived at Odiham his demeanour altered. I don't know if it was the change of scenery, the long drive to Hampshire or the end of our long walks on Salisbury Plain, but his attitude to me had taken a turn for the worse. He was listless and distant, the playfulness of the camp in Netheravon had gone.

One morning, about a week after our arrival in Hampshire, I was returning Ripper to his kennel when I noticed his body stiffening and his eyes taking on a glaze. What happened after that caught me completely by surprise.

Suddenly Ripper attacked me with all his considerable force. He knocked me to the ground and sank his teeth into my arms, legs and chest, making deep wounds in each area. The pain was excruciating and I cried out. As if he'd suddenly realised what he'd done, Ripper jumped away. When I struggled to my feet, dazed and bleeding, he came over to me, his tail wagging in that familiar friendly way. He then began licking the blood from my arm and leg. It was as if he had no memory of what had just happened.

I was soon joined by a colleague who had witnessed the attack. We both felt he must have had a fit or something similar. It was as if he had become a different dog for a few seconds.

I had to spend several days in the camp hospital while my wounds were treated. Ripper, predictably, was confined to his kennels.

When we returned to Netheravon, my superiors called me in to deliver the news that I'd been secretly dreading. Ripper and I were no longer going to the Far East. Even worse, they had decided that my dog was simply too dangerous and he would have to be put to sleep.

I was devastated. Ripper and I had worked so hard together, and I'd thought we'd achieved so much. I had never experienced euthanasia before and dreaded the prospect of saying goodbye to the dog that I still regarded as my best friend. When I was told that I would have to take him to the vet to oversee the administration of the lethal injection I felt physically sick.

The following morning I took him out of his kennel for the last time. As we walked past the long line of kennels containing barking dogs, Ripper was quiet. Normally he would have met fire with fire and barked back. It was as if he sensed what was going to happen.

He remained docile in the surgery. He let me put a muzzle on him and lift him up on to the table. The vet administered the injection quickly and cleanly. Within seconds Ripper was dead.

I am not someone who is easily moved to tears. And over the years I have watched many, many animals be put to sleep without feeling overly emotional. But that day I walked out on to the open expanse of Salisbury Plain and privately sobbed my heart out.

My colleagues were sympathetic. An investigation was carried out into the incident at Odiham, but no real conclusions were reached. Some felt he was schizophrenic, others thought he had reacted to the long night shifts, and some, like me, felt he remained badly scarred by the mistreatment he had suffered in his younger days. None of us knew for sure.

What I did know was that he had gone. We had had two wonderful months together, and I could console myself in the knowledge they may have been the happiest months of Ripper's all-too-short life.

The remaining five handlers posted to the Far East set off for Singapore a couple of days later. I was reassigned to the job of collecting German shepherds that had been donated to the RAF by the public, crisscrossing the country in the process. Every new dog I met reminded me of Ripper.

When the next training course began, I was paired up with a new dog, Rusty. He was, it's fair to say, as far removed from Ripper as it's possible to imagine. He was obedient, disciplined and easy to work with. We passed the training course without a hitch. When it came to the interview to decide my posting, I anticipated Rusty and me heading off somewhere exotic, if not the Far East, then perhaps Africa or the Mediterranean. But my posting officer had a surprise for me.

'Corporal Harper, you will be going to RAF Trerew.'

Trerew? I said to myself. Trerew in Cornwall? But that's only eight miles from home.

I must admit I had very mixed feelings boarding the train and heading back west. My posting at Trerew involved night work once more. Each night Rusty and I would walk the perimeter of the camp and check the hangars and outbuildings. It wasn't the most exciting work. But after a short time billeted on the base, I was able to get myself a 'living out' pass and return home. As I spent my days on the beach and at the local riding school, indulging my passion for horses, my love of Cornwall deepened – and the painful memory of Ripper faded slightly.

In the years that followed I often wondered what would have happened to me if Ripper hadn't attacked me that day. There's every chance we would have gone to Singapore together. I may never have found my way back to Cornwall. And my life may have turned out very differently indeed.

The morning after my meeting with Doug and Alan was a glorious one. At six o'clock the heat was so strong the air was shimmering on the road surface and was thick with the distinctive, nutty scent of gorse flowers. The light was so intense the Cornish countryside seemed alive with colour. In the marshes, there were flashes of blues as the swallows and martins hawked for insects amid the reeds. Along the hedgerows, the golden yellows of the gorse, the vivid purples of the tall loosestrife and the pinks, reds and whites of the valerian that flowered in the walls were so brilliant they almost dazzled you. I set off on my round quietly determined to face up to the German shepherd that had been terrorising Alan.

The address was a smallholding, isolated at the bottom of a valley with a small stream running along it. I approached the gate with care. There was a sign: 'NO TRESPASSERS. GUARD DOG.'

No sooner had I lifted the latch on the gate than a large, black German shepherd appeared. It came belting round from the back garden, hackles raised, seemingly intent on enjoying his daily excitement.

I had thought about this on the way here. My approach was going to be determined by the age and training of the dog. If it was an older dog, perhaps one that had been trained as a guard dog, I would have to exercise great care. If it was a younger one, a dog of a year or two, I would have more latitude. To my relief, I quickly saw that it was a very young dog, probably no older than nine or ten months. Emboldened, I dropped my postbag to the ground. I then ran headlong towards the dog waving my arms and shouting curses at the top of my voice.

My experience with poor old Ripper and various other German shepherds in the RAF had taught me that dogs of this age are acting purely out of bravado. He didn't know how to back the threat up with action, and he certainly wouldn't know how to react to a challenge. Given the three options to freeze, fight or take flight, he would almost certainly ultimately choose to run away.

As I'd anticipated, the dog first simply froze in his tracks. He wasn't expecting this. He soon turned tail and ran. He circled the house twice before diving through the front door.

I had just gathered up my postbag when the dog's owner emerged from the house, looking red-faced. He began berating me, arms flailing around like a threshing machine. 'What the hell do you think you're doing frightening my guard dog like that? He was only doing his duty,' he said.

'I know. But he doesn't have to attack to stop people trespassing on your land, does he?'

'What do you mean?' he said.

I explained that German shepherds worked best as a simple deterrent. The mere fact it was there – and thanks to the large sign, potential burglars or trespassers knew it was there – was generally enough to deter unwanted intruders.

'Your dog needs training,' I said. 'He needs to know how to behave around people. It doesn't mean he can't scare robbers off, it's just that he'll be able to identify a friendly face. Otherwise he's going to end up in deep trouble. And it will be your fault.'

Slightly shame-faced, he admitted he didn't know that much about dogs. 'Wouldn't know where to begin,' he admitted.

'I'll help you out, if you like,' I said, feeling sympathy more for the dog than the owner. We made arrangements for me to pop round one evening after work.

Back at the sorting office that afternoon, I broke the news to Alan. 'I don't think you'll be having any more trouble with that one.' I smiled.

'Really, what did you do?' he asked.

When I described what I'd done, he looked at me as if I had taken leave of my senses. He simply laughed and shook his head. 'Talk about mad dogs and Cornishmen.'

The evening after next I returned to the smallholding and started work with the German shepherd. It didn't take long to teach him the difference between right and wrong. Soon he had become a highly efficient guard dog, challenging strangers who came to his front door but leaving familiar faces – like Alan – to get on with their business in peace. The pleasure I got from helping him out was only tempered by the occasional memory of another, less fortunate dog.

'If only I'd got to Ripper this early in his life,' I said to myself quietly every now and again.

CHAPTER FOUR

The Psychedelic Parrot

The moment I stepped into the porch at the end of my morning shift at the sorting office, I knew there was something very wrong. Polly, a large scarlet macaw, was in his cage as usual, but instead of greeting me with his customary ''Ello', he was squawking gibberish and jumping animatedly around.

'What on earth's got into you?' I asked him.

When I approached the cage, Polly's reaction was an ear-splitting screech that brought Julie running out of the kitchen, a dishcloth in her hands.

'Good gracious, what's rattled his cage?' she said.

'I don't know,' I replied. 'But something definitely has.'

Polly had become a firm favourite at the cottage. He had come to us via a hotelier in Perranporth, who had bought him from a family in London, where Polly had spent his early years. No one quite knew how old Polly was. Some said he was fifty, others that he was nearer ninety. He had clearly been heavily influenced by his years in London: he spoke with a strong Cockney accent.

Polly had lived in the reception area of the hotel, where he'd been chained by one leg to a stand. Perhaps it was his Cockney accent, perhaps it was his distinctive red plumage and long tail, but for some reason he'd been teased a lot by visitors and had become distrustful and occasionally vicious towards those who came too near his cage.

At first I'd been asked to look after him while the hoteliers took a holiday themselves. But then they'd acquired some newer birds and asked me if I'd like to keep him. I'd become very attached to him so agreed.

Polly had settled down well at the cottage. He loved the sunshine and freedom of the garden and had found himself a favourite spot at the top of a conifer I had stripped down to its trunk and bare branches. It was an ideal place for a parrot to climb.

Like so many parrots, he was hugely entertaining. He would get people's attention by shouting, ''Ello,' in his thick Cockney accent. He would then begin his routine, hanging on the bars of his cage and swinging his body from side to side like a clock pendulum. 'Look at that,' he'd shout. ''Ow clever.'

His other favourite phrase was one he delivered when drinking milk. Carefully and methodically Polly would lap from a teaspoon that he'd hold in place with his foot. When the last drop of milk had disappeared, Polly would theatrically drop the spoon, wipe his beak across his perch and exclaim, 'Lovely.'

All was clearly not lovely today, however.

I left him in peace for a while, assuming that perhaps it was human company that was upsetting him today. But when I returned from the garden, an hour or so after first noticing his strange mood, he was if anything even more agitated.

He was not usually the most active of birds, but now he was jabbering away and laughing to himself like some old drunk on the streets. He was clearly alert, however. The moment I put my face near the bars of the cage he let out that awful screech, then lunged at me as if he wanted to peck out my eyes.

I was alarmed and not a little upset. I decided to call a vet friend with a specialism in birds. His was an opinion I truly respected.

But even he was baffled. 'Sounds odd. To be honest, it's not something I've come across, Rex,' he said. 'Keep an eye on him, and if he hasn't calmed down by lunchtime tomorrow, I'll come over and have a look.'

My inability to work out what was wrong with Polly was particularly annoying. Birds were, after all, my speciality. And of all the types of birds I'd dealt with over the years, the parrot family was one of those I thought I knew best.

My fascination with exotic birds had begun with a couple of mynah birds I'd taken in. I'd been amazed at their ability to copy the human voice. In one, rather sad instance, a mynah had been given to me by his widowed owner. She and her husband had adored the bird, who had been able to copy the husband's voice perfectly. When he had passed away, however, his widow had simply been unable to bear hearing his voice being mimicked by the mynah and had given the bird to me to be rehomed. The bird's name was Sparky and he was certainly a lively performer.

He was something of a pessimist, though. His favourite phrase, which he repeated time and time again, was 'It looks like rain.'

For sheer fascination, however, it was hard to match the parrot. I'd handled quite a few parrots, macaws and cockatoos over the years, most of them wild ones that had failed to settle into human homes. This, I'd learned, was one of the big problems with this type of bird. While a few were bred specifically as pets, most of the birds found in pet shops had been captured from the wild – usually when they were adults. It is extremely difficult to tame a bird like this, so as a result many suffered horrendously. It wasn't difficult to imagine the stress the birds endured when, having been wrenched from their natural habitat, they were then crammed into tiny holding boxes and transported thousands of miles to a completely alien climate and environment. To me, it was little surprise that those who survived that ordeal – and many didn't – had difficulty interacting with humans. Was it any wonder they reacted badly when they were faced with creatures who poked and prodded them, then expected them to entertain them by mimicking their speech?

For this reason I'd always tried to give the parrots, macaws and cockatoos we had in the cottage as much freedom as possible. This, of course, brought risks. One grey parrot we had was so happy in the cottage he would walk around the floor playing with the children's toys. Occasionally he would be stalked by one of our cats, but it wasn't a problem. The parrot always seemed to know where the cats were. When it detected one stalking it, it would look around and say, 'Now, then,' in a terrible voice that completely unnerved the cat.

But we also had birds who simply couldn't cope. Most parrots are gregarious by nature and to be removed from mates and flock members was more than many could endure. Some just faded away, unable to cope with solitary life in a cage. Some plucked themselves bare of feathers through boredom or nerves.

One unusual parrot we gave a home to had picked his feathers for an entirely different reason – he was addicted to cigarette smoke. The bird had lived in the bar of a pub. Over the years he had absorbed so much smoke from countless cigarettes and pipes that his plumage was covered with nicotine stains. He was also hooked on chewing up cigarettes, so when he came to us he would carefully remove a feather and sit for hours chewing it. It was only when he'd completely moulted his old plumage and spent some time with other parrots in an outside aviary that he kicked the habit.

Of the exotic birds, macaws had always been one of my favourites. Every one that had passed through our hands at the Rosery had been a great character. Macaws are big, powerful creatures with incredibly strong beaks, designed for cracking Brazil nuts, yet they are very gentle birds too. I once took in a large blue-and-gold female macaw. At the same time I was looking after a dozen lavender finches that had arrived at a local pet shop in poor condition and needed a bit of care and attention. Thinking there would be no problem, I caged the finches in the same heated bird room as the macaw. To my consternation, however, when I checked on them after their first night there was no sign of the finches in their cage. How had they escaped? And had they somehow got into the macaw's cage? If they had, what had the macaw done to them? I asked myself. She can't have gobbled them all up. Can she?

My panic didn't last long. When the macaw shuffled inside her cage, I noticed a couple of little tail feathers poking out from underneath her. I got the macaw to move and discovered all ten finches huddled there. The macaw had been brooding over them, like a hen caring for her chicks. All the finches were fine; indeed, they already looked better for their night under the macaw's feathers.

Given all these experiences and the fondness I'd developed

for macaws, I was really concerned for Polly and spent much of the night wondering about what had put him in such a strange state. The following morning I resolved to ask the vet to call at lunchtime if Polly were no better. Before I had a chance to assess Polly's condition properly, however, I got an unexpected visit from Trevor, a local policeman.

Trevor was a great animal lover and often dropped in to see who I had in residence. In the past he'd taken a cat home with him. This time, he said he was interested in a dog for his nephew. As he walked out of the porch into the garden Trevor couldn't help but notice Polly. Throughout the previous evening poor Polly had got worse and things certainly hadn't improved overnight. As Trevor stood looking at him, Polly was still dashing around like a lunatic, emitting those ear-splitting screeches.

'Haven't got a clue what's wrong with him, Trevor,' I said apologetically. 'Been like this for two days now.'

'Hmmm,' said Trevor, looking around the porch and nodding quietly to himself. 'Not normal for a macaw to be behaving like that.'

To my bemusement, he then started sniffing at the leaves of some of the plants adjacent to Polly's cage. The porch was alive with plants. All around Polly's cage in particular was an abundance of blooms, including a large Ipomoea, or morning glory.

'What are you doing, Trevor?' I asked.

His reply didn't come immediately.

'I've got a funny feeling I might know what it is,' he said eventually, removing a leaf from the morning glory. 'Does he ever eat these?' Trevor asked, handing me the leaf.

'Er, yes, I think he does sometimes,' I replied. 'Why?'

'We had a chap come in and talk to us about this not long ago. Do you know what happens if you chew the leaves or flowers of the Ipomoea, Rex?' Trevor asked, a thin smile spreading across his face.

'No.'

'Well, a lot of people in Mexico and South America use it like a drug. They chew it, then go on a psychedelic trip,' he said.

'What?'

'Like taking LSD,' Trevor said. 'It makes them as high as a kite.'

My face must have been a picture. My jaw had probably hit the floor tiles. The vine was easily reachable through the bars of his cage. Polly must have been pulling chunks off and chewing away at them.

'Well, I never,' I said eventually.

'I think your Polly has been on a bit of a trip,' Trevor said, by now chuckling to himself. 'And he didn't even have to leave his cage. If I were you, I'd move your morning glory, Rex. In fact I'd get rid of it altogether before anything else starts munching on it,' he added, with a glance at the variety of animals on display in the garden sheds.

'Don't worry, Trevor, I'll do it right away,' I said.

That afternoon I set about making sure the porch was cleared of the morning glory. Sure enough, Polly was soon showing signs of his old self. His body language was much calmer, and his incessant talking had stopped, as had his screeching. As I carried the morning glory out into the garden, he threw me a glance as if to congratulate me – and of course Trevor – on correctly diagnosing the problem.

''Ow clever,' he squawked.

CHAPTER FIVE

The Puppies That Came in From the Cold

In the morning gloom, the farmyard was still bathed in shadow, the outbuildings silent apart from the odd bleating of a ewe. As I walked towards the light of the farmhouse, however, the small collie lying alongside a wall was hard to miss. She was a bitch and, to judge by the plaintive whimpering, in some distress. Kneeling down to inspect her more closely, I quickly saw the cause. Her feet were in a terrible state. They were raw and bleeding, and seemed to be missing at least one claw.

I'd been delivering mail to the farm for quite a while now and was on speaking terms with the farmer, so when I noticed him emerging from the side of the house and heading towards the outbuildings, I called out.

I knew from experience that while many farmers had a high regard for their working animals, many others, particularly those from the older generation, did not. I wasn't surprised to discover that this one was a member of the old school.

I asked him what had happened to the collie, pointing at the dog in the yard. It was clearly not a pressing matter; indeed, he seemed surprised to see the collie there.

'Oh, her,' he said. 'She's new here. Wasn't in good shape when we got her.'

In a matter-of-fact tone, he went on to tell me how he'd bought her at a farm sale and transported her home, tied up in the boot of his car. Somehow the boot had burst open and the dog had jumped out, clearly attempting to run away. Instead she had been dragged behind the car on her paws for goodness knows how long. The farmer had driven on oblivious, until an onlooker signalled to him to stop.

It was obvious to me the dog was in serious need of treatment by a vet, but the owner had other ideas. 'Oh, she'll get over it on her own,' he said dismissively.

I couldn't countenance the collie remaining there in this state, so tried a different tack. 'She'll be ready for work that much sooner if you sort her feet out. Otherwise she'll be no use to you,' I said.

The tactic paid off. After a few moments' thought he agreed to me collecting her after I finished my round. That afternoon I carried the poor collie all the way back to the Rosery, a good three-quarters of a mile away. Her name, I'd discovered, was Nell.

Julie was up to her neck in laundry when I arrived home

cradling the new arrival. With all the animals we were taking care of, space was already at a premium not just in the garden but around the house too. This morning there were half a dozen assorted dogs and cats lounging around, so she would have been quite within her rights to blow her top at the sight of yet another four-legged lodger.

But that wouldn't have been Julie. The moment she saw the extent of Nell's wounds, she put the washing to one side and began running a bowl of water. Together we spent the next hour painstakingly washing away the dried blood and tissue that had accumulated on Nell's paws.

Nell sat there bravely throughout, only flinching now and again. As we cleaned Nell's paws up, Julie and I could see that two of her claws had been torn out and the skin on the majority of her pads was missing. She must have been in excruciating pain.

When we had finished, we dried Nell off and let her curl up on the mat in front of the Aga, where she fell asleep almost instantly. To judge by the depth of her slumber, it was the first good sleep she'd had in an age. The dog had clearly been suffering horribly for days. If she'd been left to 'get over it' herself, she may have developed all sorts of infections and ultimately been left crippled. I had no doubt her owner would have had no use for her then.

The next morning I told the farmer we'd keep her until the pads began to heal. Once more, he couldn't have cared less. 'Just be sure to bring her back when she's ready to earn a proper crust and do some work,' he said gruffly.

The way Julie had accepted this latest arrival only served to remind me how incredibly lucky I was to have her sharing my life. I couldn't imagine any other woman putting up with so many waifs and strays landing on her doorstep on an almost daily basis, especially with a young family to raise. The truth was, she was as fascinated by animals as I was – well, almost.

We'd met at the riding school where I helped out during my free time from RAF Trerew. I was a serious, solitary young man, very much a loner. So even though there were quite a few teenage girls at the riding school, none of them had really caught my eye. I had taken one or two to the pictures, but in truth I wasn't really interested, preferring to dedicate my time to training dogs at the RAF station or birdwatching on the cliffs near St Agnes, a couple of miles west of Perranporth.

Julie, however, was different. She was an apprentice hairdresser in Perranporth, but there was nothing vain or superficial about her. She wore no make-up and was very down to earth. She seemed to radiate personality. She had curly blonde hair, a lovely pair of legs, exceedingly blue eyes and a ready smile. Whenever we met at the stables, conversation seemed to come naturally between us. I fell for her the moment I set eyes on her, I think.

As I got to know her, I learned she had spent much of her childhood in India, where her now-retired father had been an army major. Like me, she'd had a great love of animals since childhood, not just horses but dogs and cats as well, and she never tired of talking about her ginger-and-white tomcat, Sunny.

A week or so after we first met I summoned up the courage to ask her out on a date. I took the plunge one morning when we were collecting horses that had been grazing overnight in the fields. I asked her whether she fancied seeing Dirk Bogarde in his new film *Doctor in the House* in Newquay that evening. To my delight, she said yes immediately. We spent the rest of the day together, chatting away virtually non-stop. We then popped home, got changed and took the train to Newquay. It turned out to be a highly memorable evening.

The film ran on for longer than I'd expected and we missed the last train back. There was a bus back as far as the village of Cubert, halfway between Newquay and Perranporth. We got off there, then set off on the four-mile march back home, picking our way through the dunes, our path illuminated by the greenish-white light of the coast's glow-worms. It must have been particularly arduous for Julie, who, in her wisdom, had come out for the evening wearing a pair of open-toed sandals. They were hardly the right footwear for the sometimes rough vegetation we had to pick our way through, but she didn't complain.

Having found a telephone en route to warn her parents of her lateness, we made it to her home around midnight. It hadn't been the most auspicious of dates, at least as far as I was concerned. I felt I'd let her down badly in making her walk home. I then compounded things by attempting to kiss her goodnight. My clumsy attempt at a peck on the cheek failed miserably. As I closed my eyes and leaned over, I not only missed her lips but I somehow failed to connect with her at all and almost fell forward flat on my face. I headed home convinced that was it, I'd blown my one and only chance with her.

To my amazement, however, when I bumped into her the next day in Perranporth, she told me what a wonderful time she'd had. What's more, she told me she'd actually turned down a date with an RAF officer in favour of a night out with me. We agreed to go out again one night.

From then on we were inseparable. Her mother was a little concerned at how serious we became, mainly because of our ages. Julie was sixteen, nearly seventeen; I was a mere nineteen. But everyone sensed it would be hard work keeping us apart.

Unfortunately, the RAF was capable of splitting us up. In

1954 I was told I was being posted to Germany. I knew I had to act quickly, so I raided my savings and headed to the nearest jeweller's, then took Julie out on to the cliffs above St Agnes to propose to her. We sat together on a precarious ledge, the fulmars wheeling effortlessly in the air above us, the sea below crashing into the cliffs.

Julie said yes almost instantly, but then – once more – I messed things up when slipping on her ring. It turned out to be much too big for her dainty little fingers and fell straight back off again, rolling on to the edge of the cliff. My heart almost jumped out of my chest as it spun there in slow motion. Thankfully, Julie stretched out a hand and grabbed it before it fell into the sea.

Our parents weren't terribly sure about the news of our engagement. Julie's mother suggested, rather wisely, that we wait until I had done my first tour of duty in Germany, by which time Julie would almost have reached her eighteenth birthday. If we still felt the same way about each other then, they would give their blessing to our marriage. I'm sure they imagined our affections would cool while I was away. It was quite the opposite. We wrote to each other almost daily, and when I returned to Cornwall in January 1956, we wasted no time in tying the knot.

The wedding took place just three days after Julie's eighteenth birthday on a cold and windy morning in a beautiful old church at Perranzabuloe. The service started at nine o'clock in the morning, an unheard-of time for weddings. But Julie and I had so little time to share before I had to return to Germany that every hour was precious. By having the service early, we gained an extra day together, or so we reckoned.

The wedding was a quiet affair. We both disliked dressing up and all the fuss and palaver of large weddings, so we turned up at the church with my mother and Julie's parents, Julie's brother and a few family friends. Julie hadn't wanted to wear a big bridal gown, but she looked absolutely lovely nevertheless dressed in a blue tweed suit and a tight-fitting feather hat. I was wearing a Burtons suit, which I had bought off the hook on my way down to Cornwall through London.

Low key it may have been, but our wedding was an unforgettable day for us both. A friend, the Reverend Harvey, officiated, and as we stood together at the altar rail in front of him, the sun suddenly broke through the heavy grey sky, sending a beam of light slanting through the stained-glass window to shine on the three of us. Was it a good omen? I like to think so. We've certainly been blessed with a wonderful marriage.

With the formalities over, we had a small reception at my mother's house in Bolingey, then headed off on our honeymoon. It wasn't the longest of trips. We honeymooned in Newquay on what we both agreed was the coldest week of the year. But we couldn't have been happier.

The only cloud hanging over us was the thought of being separated again when I headed back to Germany. Fortunately, I was able to get some married quarters for us on the base and so Julie joined me and we spent the last two years of my service there.

Our love of animals remained the thing that bound us closest together. While I spent my days working with dogs once more, Julie would occasionally get calls from people who were having problems with their pets, usually kittens or puppies. She excelled at looking after animals like this, displaying amazing levels of patience, care and ingenuity.

So when we moved back to Cornwall in 1958 and set up our first home in the caravan in Bolingey, it was no surprise that we were soon caring for everything from orphaned lambs and day-old Pekinese puppies to fox cubs and ferrets. No challenge was too great for her. She was always positive that she could help.

She put up with my whims too. I had put my name down for a job at the post office but in the meantime was working in a woollen mill in Truro. Once, I returned home from work with a new dog in tow. I'd bought him from a local farmer without consulting Julie. When I arrived in the caravan with the dog, our first cat, a Siamese called Sabi, flew straight into the air, terrified. She then landed on Julie's back, plunging her claws into her. The look Julie gave me almost turned me to stone, but when she saw the new arrival standing there, his tail wagging with joy at the sight of his new co-owner, her face quickly softened.

'Who's your handsome friend, then?' she said, leaning down to ruffle the dog's neck.

Since our move to the Rosery, and as our small sanctuary had grown, it had been Julie's positive outlook that had kept us going. While I was prone to seeing problems, Julie always saw the glass as half full. I regarded her, quite simply, as the wind beneath my wings.

Winter was setting in outside, and as we sat in the living room, Julie and I had pulled our chairs close to the log fire. Suddenly, against the crackle of the burning wood and the howling of the wind in the chimney, we heard a strange scratching at the front door. We exchanged puzzled looks, then walked to the door together.

We were both taken aback by the sight that greeted us. There, on the doorstep, was Nell, the injured collie whose feet we had treated just a few weeks back. She was carefully clutching what looked like a day-old puppy in her teeth.

Once she had healed, I had, somewhat reluctantly, taken Nell back to the farm. Since then I'd seen her occasionally during my deliveries. She had never looked particularly healthy. She had seemed underfed, with her ribs visible. The last time I'd seen her, however, I'd noticed she was pregnant. I'd felt concerned for her and had wondered what would happen to her litter if, as was likely to be the case, they were unwanted.

Clearly Nell had felt the same way – hence her visit to us.

'Hello, Nell. Who's this you've got with you?' Julie said, stroking her gently on the back of the neck. 'You'd better bring the little one in.'

This was obviously the reaction she'd hoped for. Nell walked into the living room and placed her tiny offspring on the same spot she'd slept on her first night with us, the mat by the Aga. She immediately turned, ran straight back out of the front door and into the night.

Julie and I looked at each other in amazement. We then set about finding a box and a blanket for the puppy. Barely half an hour had passed when there was a scratching at the door again. It was Nell with another puppy in her mouth. She trotted in, deposited her on the mat and turned on her heels. Over the next couple of hours Nell repeated this operation three more times. Each time she was obviously running the three-quarters of a mile back to the farm, picking up a puppy, then carefully carrying it across the fields to the Roscry. By the end of the evening we had five young puppies piled up together in a box in the corner of the kitchen. Nell spent the night with them, allowing them to suckle from her.

As the sanctuary had grown, Julie and I had taken a quiet pride in what we were doing. In our hearts, we felt we'd provided a good temporary home for a variety of waifs and strays and that we'd set them on their way towards, hopefully, a good life. But deep down we weren't sure whether what we were doing was the right thing. Nell changed all that.

Clearly she had remembered the Rosery as somewhere she had felt safe when she'd been recovering from her injuries. Now she was a mother, she'd gone to the trouble of bringing her family here to enjoy the same combination of safety and warmth. As far as we were concerned, we couldn't have been paid a higher compliment. Times weren't easy, nor, with money and time tight at every turn, were they likely to get any easier. At moments like this, however, that didn't seem to matter. The sacrifices we were making were all worthwhile.

That morning, looking down on the basket of five vulnerable puppies, I couldn't help thinking to myself, We must be doing something right.

The puppies stayed with us for eight weeks or so and then returned to the farm with their mother. Fortunately for them all, the old farmer was handing over the running of the place to his son and his young family. They had a much more enlightened attitude to dogs, and all but one of the puppies was found a new home. The remaining one, a male, lived on the farm with Nell, and became, like his mother, a well-cared-for family pet.

CHAPTER SIX
A Lost Cause

The isolated bungalow had been empty for many weeks – and looked it. The overgrown garden was strewn with all manner of rubbish: old mattresses, piles of empty tins and bottles, small mountains of cardboard boxes and paper. The air was heavy with the smell of decaying food.

Some passers-by had called us. They were concerned about a cat that had been seen pawing at the windows trying to get inside. It was apparently in quite a bad way physically and seemed distressed too. All attempts to capture it had failed. It was nervous and prone to lashing out at anyone who went near it.

I'd managed to trace the owner of the property and

discovered it had been let to a couple who had done a moonlight flit, owing him months of rent and, it would seem, abandoning their pet. The owner had given me permission to go over to the bungalow to check on the cat.

Picking my way towards the bungalow, I began by calling out to the cat. There was no harm in trying, I told myself. Cats react differently to different voices. It might respond to mine. There was no sign of movement in or around the front of the house, however, so I headed round the back into the rear garden.

The back was in an even worse state than the front, completely overgrown and run-down. Half concealed amidst the bramble and elder, I spotted a shed of rusty, galvanised metal, full of holes. Over the doorway, the rotted wooden lintel had split in two and had dropped almost to the ground. Crawling inside the narrow entrance, I was suddenly hit by the overpowering stench of decomposing flesh. It seemed to be coming from the far corner of the shed, where some old rags were strewn out across the floor. Peeling away the rags, I found a very young dead kitten. It was horribly emaciated and looked no older than a few days, perhaps a week or two at the most. It had probably been born in this wretched place.

I turned to scan the rest of the shed floor. Almost immediately I saw a second kitten, again dead, lying in another corner. Like its sibling, it looked as if it had died within days of being born. It, too, was little more than decaying skin and bones.

Clearly there was nothing I could do for the kittens. From the description the caller had given me, however, there was still a chance I could find what I now assumed was their mother. Sure enough, as I left the grim scene and headed back towards the house, I glimpsed a cat sitting beneath a small kitchen window. In reality, it was more like the *ghost* of a cat. Her tortoiseshell fur was sticking out stiffly from a thin, skeletal body, her sunken eyes were staring up at the glass, and her mouth was open, as if ready to call out, but she was so weak and lacking in energy no sound came.

Inwardly I could feel my blood boiling at the irresponsibility of the couple who had run away from their duties here. Pulling myself together, I reminded myself I had a job to do. I approached the cat, speaking softly to her. I had on heavy gloves and was armed with a cat basket and a blanket in case she got violent. But neither was needed. Without any great difficulty I picked her up and placed her in the basket. As I did so, I noticed she had a nametag round her neck. She was called Tilly.

Many people assume that domestic cats are capable of fending for themselves. Clearly this is what this cat's owners had assumed, although I doubt they'd really given her fate a moment's thought. The truth, however, is that some cats are better at surviving on their own than others. While some can get by preying on mice and birds and even rabbits, others can't. Evidently Tilly hadn't been able to. The timing of her abandonment could not have been worse. Judging from the corpses of the kittens, the cat had probably been left to fend for herself during the final stages of her pregnancy. I doubted these owners would even have known it.

My guess was that Tilly had been so run-down by the time she gave birth she probably had no milk in her teats to feed her newborns. I'm sure she would have stayed with them, licking and cleaning them. But the hard fact was that they had not been able to live on love alone.

I took Tilly home with a heavy heart.

I placed her in a cage in our cattery, under the warm glow of an infrared lamp, but she couldn't settle and relax. All that day and night she paced up and down her cage on stiff legs, the picture of misery. But she did eat. Julie and I fed her small, nourishing meals several times a day. We beat up raw eggs with her milk, so her condition did slowly improve, her thin body filling out and her coat taking on a healthy shine. But it was clear to us her spirit was still broken. Her eyes were dull and lacked the sparkle of life. I had always believed animals could feel grief. Looking into Tilly's eyes, I was more sure of that than ever.

Out of necessity, catching cats had become something of a speciality of mine. I continued to preach to people about spaying and neutering, but clearly I might as well have been speaking to the wall. Unwanted cats seemed to be everywhere, as did the clueless individuals who thought they were looking after their best interests.

A few weeks before finding Tilly, I'd been called out to a council estate in Newlyn East. The caller had told me about three wild cats that had become a problem and were, according to her, 'running amok'.

On arriving there late one afternoon, I had discovered the owners of the house had been encouraging a trio of strays to feed and take shelter on their porch every evening. The cats spent their days foraging on the surrounding farmland, then tucked themselves up on the porch at night. The problem was, they were eating their benefactors out of house and home. They had also proved very wary of strangers and had lashed out quite nastily at some who had approached them. The lady who called us had had enough.

After reviewing the situation, I'd come up with a plan to draw the cats into a small scullery behind the porch where we would be able to shut them in. I would then be able to go in with my normal cat-catching kit: a cat basket, a blanket and a pair of thick gloves. All was proceeding according to plan until the lady's husband appeared. Seeing the three cats in the scullery and me getting ready to catch them with my gloves and blanket, he looked at me with complete scorn and pushed ahead of me.

'Gloves and blankets, never heard of such a thing,' he said, letting himself into the scullery. 'Here, I'll go and catch them. Just be sure to have your cat basket open ready to take them.'

He shut the door behind him, and, with his wife, I listened carefully.

Through the door I heard him talking to the cats. 'Come along, me 'ansomes. I'll not 'urt you. Come on now,' he said, obviously coaxing them towards him. Then suddenly there was a loud shout. 'Ow, you buggers.'

Almost immediately the door flung open to reveal the husband holding his hand, which was dripping blood. His face was white and twisted with pain.

'The buggers went for me like tigers,' he said to me. 'They're all yours, mate. Take 'em away. I never want to see 'em again.'

Unfortunately, his efforts had made my task even harder. The cats were now completely wound up. The moment I opened the door all three of them flew past me up the passage into the kitchen. I followed them into the room, where I found them going completely berserk in their attempts to get out. The only window was closed and curtained, but that didn't stop them clambering up on to the windowsill, scattering flowerpots and ornaments, then getting themselves tangled up in the net of the curtains.

When they spotted me in the room, they panicked even more and leaped in the direction of a small Welsh dresser, stacked with the family's china. As all three cats tried to clamber their way to the top of the dresser, pieces of crockery started crashing to the floor. Soon the room was filled with the noise of shattering porcelain and the shouts of the owners. 'Do something! Stop them!' the wife was screaming at me.

Sensing they would only make matters worse, I'd asked the couple to stay outside as I dealt with things. They'd not heeded my request, however, and the results were all too predictable. Rather than calming the cats, the couple's manic shouts were doing the exact opposite. The cats were now becoming even more terrified.

Suddenly the top half of the dresser detached itself from the base, toppling over and falling to the floor with a tremendous crash. The couple's shouts then turned to screams and wails of despair. This sent the panicked cats on to the next highest point in the kitchen, the draining board. The worktop was covered with saucepans containing the evening meal, all of which landed on the floor. The mess included the contents of a large pan of custard.

By now the kitchen looked like it had been hit by a bomb. The wife was hysterical and the husband frozen to the spot, blood still dripping from his hand.

At last, however, I had a chance to make my move.

The cats had finally found shelter in a small cupboard under the sink, where they were cowering, as emotionally drained as the humans in this mini drama. I moved in with my gloves and – ignoring the spits and snarls, the bites and slashing paws – lifted them one by one into separate baskets.

As I began taking the baskets out to the van, I saw that a small crowd of people had gathered outside the house. Clearly the noise must have been considerable and had drawn the neighbours out of their homes.

'Just catching some wild cats,' I said by way of explanation.

'Must have been pretty wild,' one boy said to me.

'Well, they were by the end,' I said with a rueful smile.

One or two women followed me into the house, where they consoled the husband and wife and began the lengthy task of cleaning up the mess.

I collected the last of the cats and headed back to the Rosery, having learned a few valuable lessons, not least of which was never to underestimate the stupidity and arrogance of some people when it comes to animals.

As it turned out, I was able to find a home for the three wild cats. I was in contact with a local farmer who was on the lookout for some cats to keep down the vermin population in his haylofts and cattle sheds. Once they'd been neutered, I took the terrible trio there, where they settled in almost immediately, living in an outbuilding.

Now, as Tilly settled into life at the Rosery, I hoped to find her the right home too.

It took me a few weeks to get her on the road to recovery. Then, soon after she'd returned to reasonable health, a couple called who were keen to acquire a new cat. They took one look at Tilly and asked to home her. I was delighted. After the trauma she'd been through, if any cat deserved a second chance, this one did, I thought to myself. Unfortunately, life isn't always straightforward.

It wasn't long before the new owners were on the phone to us. The home they'd provided for Tilly couldn't have been more of a contrast to the hovel in which she'd lived previously. Their cottage was set in open countryside with a log fire and lots of comfortable furniture. What was more, Tilly had got herself a pair of kind and considerate owners. They'd done all the right things in terms of settling her into her new home, keeping her in the house for the first week and then accompanying her on her first walks around the garden so as to calm her anxieties.

But Tilly wouldn't settle. One morning she had gone missing. They had searched the surrounding area calling for her but to no avail. The little cat had vanished.

When they called us, Tilly hadn't been seen for two days.

I asked them to keep an eye out for her for a few days more

and to call me at the end of the week if she hadn't returned. The week passed and still there was no sign of Tilly, so I followed a hunch and headed to the bungalow where she'd lived before.

She wasn't there the first time, but I went back repeatedly over the next few days. Sure enough, on the third or fourth day she was there, all skin and bone once more, sitting in that familiar spot under the kitchen windowsill.

I took her back to the Rosery again. As before, she ate ravenously. She drank some egg and milk, and then collapsed in an armchair, falling into a sleep of pure exhaustion. After a few days I returned her to her new owners, hoping against hope that this time she would remain there.

A couple of weeks later Julie called me to the phone, looking pale.

'It's Tilly,' she said, cupping a hand over the mouthpiece. 'She's gone again.'

This time my attempts to find her at the bungalow came to nought.

It was another fortnight before we got a phone call, this time from the new occupants of the bungalow, whom I'd met on my last visit there. They'd found a cat in a terrible condition lying underneath the kitchen window.

'What was your cat's name again?' the caller asked. 'This one's got a nametag on it.'

'Tilly,' I said.

'Yes, it's Tilly all right. Poor thing's in a heck of a state.'

By the time I arrived at the bungalow Tilly was very near death. She had probably been hit by a car. Her tail hung from her body by a mere thread of flesh, and her back was a mess of dried blood. There was nothing that I could do other than take her to the vet as quickly as I could. There, she was quietly and painlessly put to sleep.

Since we'd started taking in waifs and strays I'd known deep down that we were never going to be able to save every creature. We'd had losses and had dealt with them. For some reason, however, this one seemed harder to take in our stride. Both Julie and I were deeply upset by Tilly's death.

The question that kept going through my mind for days afterwards was, why did she return to that house? She must have sustained her injuries several days before she was discovered. The journey from her new home involved her travelling along miles of country lanes. She had dragged herself back to her former home, leaving the warmth and comfort behind, but for what? Was it love for the uncaring owners that brought her back? Was it the urge to be near her dead kittens? Or was it something simpler? Was it merely that she felt insecure away from the place where she had grown up, the home where perhaps a dish of food had been put on the kitchen windowsill for her? It was impossible to know. Sometimes animals are subject to forces beyond either our control or comprehension. But whatever the allure of that dreadful place, Tilly had answered its call until the very end.

CHAPTER SEVEN
Helping Hands

By the mid-1960s the morning ritual at the Rosery had become so familiar I could have done it in my sleep. There were days, especially during the pitch-dark winter, when I suspect I did.

I would stumble out of bed, bleary-eyed, around a quarter past five. Having first let the dogs and cats that lived in the cottage out for a run, I'd slip into my wellingtons, grab a torch and head off into the garden to do the rounds of the cages. I'd always start by checking the progress of the injured animals, treating those that needed medical attention, then moving those that had improved overnight from the hospital cages to the aviary or cattery. I would then feed and generally tend to the needs of the assorted inmates. With such a diverse collection of animals coming our way, this could involve anything from medicating a sickly rabbit with some lettuce to releasing a sparrow back into the wild.

As well as waking me up, the rounds usually put me in good spirits before I headed off to the sorting office at around a quarter past six. Today, however, the routine was only making me more and more anxious.

The feeling that things were getting slightly out of control had been creeping up on me for a while now. Conditions had always been pretty cramped at the Rosery. It was, after all, only a small cottage. We'd managed to build an extension with two bedrooms for the boys and – luxury of luxuries – an indoor toilet and bathroom. But when Julie and I had started taking in the occasional foster child, the new-found space seemed to disappear again.

The ever-expanding collection of animals we were attracting made matters even worse, of course. We invariably had around half a dozen cats and at least a couple of dogs with us at any one time. For a while they were all housed outside, but no longer. The cattery in the garden was full to the brim, so a fair few of the cats, along with all the dogs, were now resident in the house. The aviary and bird hospital, too, were chock-a-block with patients in various states of health. So many birds were crammed in there we had begun using 'overflow' facilities, sometimes literally. At one point we'd had a buzzard in the outside lavatory. The wounded bird spent two weeks living on a perch there.

The fact there was no room at the inn wasn't the only problem. A postman's wage wasn't exactly brilliant, and with two young sons to clothe and feed, a cottage to renovate and a small mortgage to meet, there wasn't much cash flying around at the end of the week. Julie had also announced that she was pregnant again. Our third child's arrival was drawing closer by the day. Feeding the animals was therefore becoming an increasing challenge. It wasn't simply a case of buying the odd tin of cat food. There were the dogs to feed, plus a wide variety of birds, many of which required special diets and medicines. On top of this, all the assorted guinea pigs, rabbits and tortoises that passed through our sanctuary needed fresh vegetables. We grew some, but never enough.

Various locals had been generous to us by making donations of food or occasionally a little money. Vets too let us have medicines at the lowest possible prices. But we could never quite make ends meet. Animals, especially young animals, have large appetites.

So it wasn't entirely a surprise when, preparing the various feeds for the animals this particular morning, I noticed that we were almost out of food for the cats and dogs. When I went through the supplies, I saw we were nearly out of bird seed too. All I had for them was a tin of mealworms, a tasty snack but hardly enough to keep the aviary residents going for long.

As I headed back to the kitchen for a mug of tea before setting off to work, I suddenly felt overwhelmed.

Julie was usually up before six too, even in her heavily pregnant condition. Often I'd have to cut my rounds short to get off to work. Over a cup of tea we'd discuss what needed doing to the various animals before I jumped on my bike and headed off to the sorting office. This morning, however, I wasn't in a very communicative mood when I returned from the garden.

'What's wrong with you?' Julie asked, picking up on my mood in an instant.

I wasn't in the right frame of mind to keep things bottled up, so I just blurted it out. 'We can't carry on like this,' I said.

'We've barely got enough money to feed and clothe the four of us, let alone look after that lot out there.'

Julie was well used to my occasional bouts of negativity, but she clearly sensed this was serious. 'Are things really that bad?'

I nodded my head in agreement for a moment. 'Afraid so,' I said eventually. 'And I don't know what we are going to feed them all on next week. I don't think they'll do very well on a diet of fresh air.'

Julie sat there quietly for a while, cradling her mug of tea in both hands as she took things in. 'There's got to be somebody who would be willing to support us. A charity or something,' she said. 'What about asking the RSPCA for some help?'

At first the suggestion sounded too far-fetched for words. 'Why would they help a tinpot little place like this?' I asked. 'They've got their hands full with their proper rescue centres.'

'Have they?' Julie said. 'I don't know of many round here. There can't be any harm in asking.'

I harrumphed around the kitchen, then headed back out again. As I did so, however, I realised she had a point. I also realised we had some contact with the charity that might help. My mother had some connections with the RSPCA. Each year she'd help the local secretary, Mrs Peebles, to organise a charity collection. I called in to see her at the end of my round. She said she'd speak to Mrs Peebles.

In truth I didn't expect anything much to happen, but – to my mild surprise – my mother turned up the next day clutching a piece of paper.

'Here's a number for the local RSPCA chief inspector,' she said. 'Give him a call. Mrs Peebles thinks he might be able to help.'

The chief inspector for Cornwall was a man called Ralph Gardner. He was based in Truro, nine or so miles away. But when I called I spoke to his wife, Jean, who it transpired took all the calls for the RSPCA in Cornwall at that time. Little did I know that our conversation would be the first of hundreds we would have over the coming years.

She was polite and to the point. 'I'd heard there was someone over near Perranporth taking in animals,' she said. 'The chief inspector was thinking of giving you a call at some point. You've saved him the bother.'

I must admit I was flattered, and a little surprised, that she'd heard about the sanctuary. What she said next, however, took me aback even more.

'The thing is,' she said, 'there isn't an RSPCA animal home in the whole of Cornwall, so we are always on the lookout for places where we can place animals that come to us. We might be able to help you out financially, give you some equipment, that sort of thing. I think the best thing is for Ralph to come over and look at your set-up and see if you can help us out.'

'Great,' I said, stuck for words.

'Next Tuesday any good?' she said.

Money and resources may have been in short supply, but with two growing boys around the house, at least we were never short of willing helpers.

Glen's most memorable moment came when we'd taken charge of an unusual part-time resident, a Magellan penguin.

The penguin had come to us from a newly set-up bird garden nearby. He had picked up a foot infection and the bird garden, nervous about treating such a rare bird, had asked me whether I could look after him while he recuperated. I was happy to do so. I got hold of the appropriate antibiotic from a vet, then housed the bird in a makeshift enclosure. I'd read much about penguins but hadn't got any closer to them than the other side of the wire at Bristol Zoo. What amazed me was how heavy this one was for his size. I had to clean and dress his foot each day and it was quite an effort to pick him up. He could also deliver a fierce bite if handled wrongly.

As he got better, however, he became much more mobile, regularly escaping from his pen to harass other creatures. It was one of these escapes that provided Glen with a bit of excitement.

One morning while I had a cup of tea after the postal round, Glen appeared breathlessly in the kitchen, clearly bursting to tell me his news.

'Dad,' he said, 'the penguin's in the fishpond eating the goldfish.'

At first I wasn't certain I believed him. But sure enough, when I dashed out to the garden I discovered the penguin finishing off the last of our small collection of goldfish.

'Thanks, Glen,' I said. Trying to extract a positive from the situation, I added, 'You did the right thing in coming to tell me. You almost saved them.'

I was relieved to return the penguin to his long-term keepers at the bird garden shortly afterwards, but the memory has never been forgotten by Glen.

Although a couple of years younger than his big brother, Alan too was a real practical help and regularly joined me as I did the daily rounds of the cages and aviaries. He had proved an excellent dog handler in particular, often volunteering to exercise the rescue dogs that came our way. He'd learned some valuable lessons, including not to get too attached to the damaged creatures that passed through our portals. This particular lesson had been delivered by a chow-chow that we had been asked to keep for a short time by a local vet. The dog had been an adult with an unkempt coat and the standoffish attitude that is typical of the breed, but Alan had fallen for him nevertheless, spending hours taking him for walks and looking after him.

However, when the chow-chow had been with us a few weeks, I'd had to take him to the vet's to be treated for a bad case of mange. The dog had gone completely haywire at the surgery, turning savagely on me and the staff there. It had been a real struggle to bring him under control and we'd reluctantly decided to put him down.

When I had contacted the vet about this, they had informed me that he had a long record of attacking people. What shook me more than the attack itself was the fact that my son had been handling such a dangerous dog. Alan had naturally been upset when I had told him that his friend would not be returning from the vet's, but it proved a lesson for both of us.

There had been many happier moments, however, not least when we took part-time care of a pony.

Alan's greatest passion was for horses, so when I arrived home one evening to announce we were to offer a part-time home to a Dartmoor pony, I thought he was going to spontaneously combust with excitement. He was ecstatic.

The pony had been bought by our friend, a local chemist, from a rather dodgy dealer for his three children. But they had quickly tired of all the work involved in caring for a pony.

Lightning, as he was known, was a dark bay gelding, twelve hands high and about four years old. There was barely any room for him in our garden, but fortunately a kindly neighbour offered to let us graze him in a nearby field.

The children loved him, and he allowed them to groom him, tack him up and ride him around the field and lanes. Alan rode Lightning most days, wearing a riding hat from under which his long, golden, wavy hair flopped loosely around. Then one day he heard a passer-by say, 'What lovely hair that Harper girl has.' I don't think a boy has ever volunteered for a haircut quite so quickly.

Lightning became popular with other children in the village

too. Whenever one of our children had a birthday party, visiting friends were given rides, bouncing along happily as they were led up and down the lane.

It wasn't all plain sailing with Lightning, though. Ponies can be strong-willed and naughty characters at times, and if Lightning decided to stop to eat an especially attractive morsel in the hedge, or climb halfway up a wall to see what was in the next field, he would do so, regardless of his young rider's efforts to control him. Julie and I fared little better when it fell to us to exercise him.

Small ponies run to fat very easily, which can lead to health problems, so it was important to make certain that Lightning had sufficient exercise. This was easy enough when the children were at home, but on schooldays it would fall to Julie or me to take him out for an hour or so.

At first Lightning resented me riding him, not because of my weight, I hasten to add. Dartmoors are tough and my ten stones meant little to him, but he was used to children and was not keen on being told what to do by a more experienced rider. To be honest, I always felt rather silly riding the little pony, as my feet just about touched the ground on either side of his stout body. And, for all my experience with horses, Lightning frequently had me over his head when I least expected his next move. I always rode him bareback and he would canter away across the field and then suddenly stop, jerking his head downwards. The suddenness of the action would take me unawares and throw me forward so that I slid down the pony's neck on to the ground. Whenever this happened Lightning would stand looking down at me with a smug expression, obviously well pleased with himself.

With Julie he employed a different tactic. He would be trotting along a lane as good as gold when all at once he would decide to look over a wall, or Cornish hedge, as we called them. Diving sideways, he would climb up the steep grass bank, causing Julie to slide off backwards.

One morning I was literally taken for a ride by the mischievous pony. It was one of those lovely bright early-summer mornings and I had decided to take Lightning to the beach. I rode him into the water and sat there looking out over the calm blue sea, completely lost in thought.

Unbeknown to me, however, four riders mounted on large hunter-type horses had ridden on to the sands behind me. When I finally spotted them, they had set the horses into a canter, which turned quickly into a gallop, and then they were off, tearing away along the three miles of beach.

Lightning had not missed the action. His ears went up, his body stiffened and before I realised what was happening the little pony had taken the bit firmly between his teeth and was galloping off in hot pursuit of the vanishing riders.

Somehow, I don't know quite how, I managed to keep my balance and remain mounted. But I had no control over the pony, and he just kept going, until, puffing and breathless, we arrived at the end of the beach, where the riders had halted and were watching our progress amid much laughter.

I slid off Lightning's back feeling shaken but had to join in the general merriment. The whole episode must have resembled a Thurber cartoon. The sight of the fat little pony with his short legs ridden by a skinny, out-of-control rider whose feet almost touched the sand would certainly have made a great video.

The children's affection for Lightning was enormous, however, and it was proven when he fell seriously ill. The trouble began when a well-intentioned person emptied a bag of lawn cuttings into Lightning's field. The passer-by clearly thought the pony would enjoy the snack, which he did. But grass cuttings are unsuitable fare, and having eaten a great deal of the pile, Lightning developed colic and was in great pain when we later discovered him, listlessly standing by the field gate and constantly raising a hind leg to kick at his aching stomach.

We managed to get the pony back to the cottage and put him in our small backyard. But by the time the vet had arrived an hour or so later, Lightning had collapsed in the tiny porch and was lying across the back door. Fortunately, the vet was able to squeeze into the porch alongside the prostrate pony and administer a drench, which, after a while, seemed to ease the pain. Even so, Lightning remained lying in the porch for two days, much to the consternation of the children, and Alan in particular.

Throughout that time it was Alan who cared for him, feeding him carefully and checking on him day and night. To our immense relief, Lightning made a full recovery. I'm not sure how Alan would have coped if he hadn't.

Sadly, we eventually had to find Lightning a new home. He developed a condition known as sweet itch, brought on each year in the late spring when midges bite the pony's mane and tail, causing an allergic reaction and an irritating itch that is only made worse by constant rubbing.

On the advice of the vet we tried rubbing sulphur ointment into the sores and covering the vulnerable areas with bandages made from torn-up sheets. But it was all to no avail. We had no stable or shed where Lightning could be put during the late evening and at night when the midges were active.

So it was that, in the end, we gave the pony to a local farmer who could provide the shelter he required. Alan and the rest of the family missed him tremendously, although they would see him every now and again walking the lanes.

* * *

A few days after my conversation with the RSPCA, I heard the sound of a vehicle pulling up outside the cottage. I popped my head out to see a very smartly uniformed man in his mid-forties emerging from one of the organisation's distinctive white vans.

'Mr Harper, Ralph Gardner. I think you spoke to my wife, Jean, on the phone,' he said, extending an arm over the gate.

Ralph Gardner turned out to be one of the most inspirational people I've ever met. The conversation we had that morning was to change my life.

He was a tall, well-built man, grey-haired with a trustworthy face. He was wearing the regulation navy-blue uniform, peaked cap, white shirt and black tie. He was quietly spoken, yet still carried a real air of authority about him. He spoke directly, not wasting his words.

'So, let's have a look at what you've got here, Mr Harper,' he said, clapping his hands together and looking in the direction of the cages he could see in the garden.

As was now the norm, the aviary and bird hospital were filled with young birds. We had a couple of lost racing pigeons and a parrot recovering from an injury. The buzzard in the loo was still in residence too. The sight of it perched over the toilet bowl brought a smile to Ralph's face.

'You weren't exaggerating when you said you were full to overflowing,' he said, smiling.

'Any port in a storm.' I shrugged.

I showed him the cattery too, which predictably sparked a conversation about the number of feral cats roaming the county.

'The bane of my life,' Ralph said, shaking his head slowly.

'If people would only take them to the vet's, we wouldn't have all this trouble,' I said.

'Exactly, Rex,' Ralph said quietly. 'But they won't listen, will they?'

As we chatted away, he was complimentary about what I was doing and interested in the stories attached to the animals I had.

'You seem to know a lot about birds. Is that your speciality?' he asked me at one point.

'I was a pigeon fancier as a boy and it kind of took off from there,' I said, smiling at the pun. As it turned out, Ralph wasn't a man with a great sense of humour. The joke flew over his head, as it were.

The tour didn't take long. Afterwards he came into the kitchen for a cup of tea. We chatted for fully an hour.

'The trouble with a lot of people who start doing what you do is they get too sentimental,' he said, shaking his head ruefully. 'Not every story has a happy ending. But some people don't want to hear that.'

Ralph's view reflected the official policy of the RSPCA, which understood that some domestic animals were simply not suitable to be passed on as pets and couldn't be kept indefinitely.

'It's tough, I know, but sometimes euthanasia is the best solution,' he said.

I understood entirely what he meant. Every now and again Julie and I had probably been guilty of clinging on to an animal when we shouldn't have done. But I knew he was right.

Ralph explained a little of the formalities that would have to be carried out if we were to become involved with the RSPCA. To be honest, I didn't really tune in. I was taken aback slightly that he was talking in these terms.

'So you think you might be able to help us, then?' I said.

'Yes, sorry. I should have said. Yes, this is definitely the sort of set-up we would want to support, Mr Harper,' he said. 'There aren't anywhere near enough places like this in the county.'

He went on to explain that he would talk about his visit to the Rosery at the next meeting of the county's RSPCA committee.

'I'll let everyone know what a sterling job you are doing here and then ask them to put their hands in their pockets.' He smiled.

He explained that he was going to put our names up for a grant, or honorarium. It wasn't going to be a huge sum of money, but it would be significant enough to cover a lot of our outgoings.

'I will propose we get you some funds to build an extra cattery as well,' he said, looking around the kitchen at the collection of cats draped, it seemed, across every piece of furniture. 'I'm sure your wife would like to have her kitchen back.'

CHAPTER EIGHT

An Otter on the Aga

With more and more people knocking on our door for help, I was learning a great deal – and not just about animals.

One lesson I'd understood early on, for instance, was to take some people's emergency calls with a healthy pinch of salt. It wasn't that our callers weren't well intentioned. They invariably were. It was just that their vivid descriptions of injured animals didn't always fit the realities that revealed themselves when I headed off to the scene.

Recently, for instance, I'd had a man call up to report a duck that was 'covered in blood'. I'd headed off expecting perhaps to find the victim of a fox attack or a road accident. Instead I discovered a Muscovy duck, with its distinctive scarlet-coloured skin round its eyes, sitting on a riverbank preening itself as if it didn't have a care in the world.

So when a local lady rang early one morning claiming she had seen an otter stranded and crying out in distress on the nearby river Allen, I initially had my doubts. First of all, I doubted very much the animal she had seen was an otter. They had for many years been a rare sight in Cornwall. And while there had been a recent growth in their numbers, the sad truth was that the only ones that came our way were dead ones, victims of road accidents more often than not. Besides, it was hard to imagine an otter getting into trouble in water, its natural habitat. As I headed for the spot on the river the lady had described, my guess was that I was going to find a mink. Mink had been turning up in all sorts of unlikely spots in recent times. Perhaps this one had somehow got itself into trouble.

The place where the 'otter' had been seen was about nine miles from Bolingey, at a point where the river Allen, a tributary of the larger river Fal, curved its way through a small hamlet at the foot of a wooded valley. It only took a moment for me to see that stranded on a rock in the middle of the fast-flowing river was an otter cub. It couldn't have been much more than eight weeks old. It was lying on its side and calling out weakly. If there had been any humble pie to hand, I would have had to eat a very large slice of it that morning. The lady had described the situation entirely accurately.

The river Allen was in flood and was rising even now. My suspicion was that the waters had reached such a level that they had somehow washed this cub out of its holt further up the river and carried it downstream, where it had come to rest on these rocks. Even from my vantage point on the bank I could see the otter was so weak and cold it wasn't going to last very much longer. Luckily the flood waters hadn't completely consumed the landscape and there were still several large rocks protruding from the river. I scrambled my way across them and quickly grabbed the cub.

Back on the bank, I saw that the otter was in an even more fragile state than I'd imagined, shivering violently. It was icy cold to the touch. I suspected the nine-mile journey home was going to be too much for it, but I had to try. With a towel I dried some of the water from its dripping fur. I then placed the tiny animal inside my shirt, with its freezing body pressed tight up under my armpit. It lay there trembling as I carefully drove home.

Goodness knows what Julie must have thought when I walked into the kitchen, fished inside my soggy shirt and produced the sopping-wet baby otter. To be honest, at this point, she had more important things to worry about.

Our third child, Klair, was now a couple of months old. She'd arrived in the world upstairs, at four thirty on a Thursday afternoon in February 1966, weighing in at six and a half pounds. She had already proven a delightful baby with a mass of dark hair and a happy, calm nature. The experience of being a mother clearly agreed with Julie. She was already expecting again, although neither of us was quite sure how this had come about. Julie blamed the postman.

With Klair asleep in her crib, Julie was soon taking an interest in the creature I was trying to dry out near the Aga.

'Let me have a look,' she said.

Over the years, Julie had proven herself to be an expert at rearing all kinds of animals. She'd successfully nurtured everything from day-old Pekinese puppies to sickly lambs and calves. Nothing seemed to faze her. This time, however, the look on her face as she was handed a three-quarters dead otter cub was telling. It said, 'What on earth do I do with this?'

'It might be too far gone,' I said, reassuring her. 'Don't worry if you can't do anything.'

Julie wasn't one to mull things over for long. She gave a shrug of her shoulders, muttered something to herself and then headed off into the larder with the otter still tucked under her arm. I heard the crashing of various objects. Julie soon emerged with a small cardboard box and a towel.

To my bemusement, Julie headed to the Aga, where she proceeded to open one of the side doors.

'What are you going to do, cook it?' I asked, unable to bite my tongue this time. The look Julie gave me should by rights have turned me into a pillar of salt.

With the weather warming up, Julie had begun turning the temperature of the oven down. It wasn't hot enough to cook anything, but it was a perfect environment to keep things warm. And perhaps to revive an otter.

'Let's give it half an hour or so in there and see what happens,' Julie said, carefully sliding the box into the oven, leaving the door open.

Sure enough, within half an hour the otter had revived markedly. It had started to stretch its legs and it seemed to be calmer. Its breathing had also improved hugely.

'Let me get an infrared lamp,' I said, heading out into the aviary.

'All right,' Julie replied. 'I'll see if I can sort out something for this chap to eat.'

I returned to see Julie feeding the cub with a syringe containing glucose and water. She had also prepared a mixture of a special puppy-rearing milk substitute, Lactol, which can be used on some animals other than dogs. She had mixed this with raw, flaked fish. Julie's flair for feeding small animals never ceased to amaze me. The otter was capable of lapping and soon began happily consuming the mixture off the end of a spoon.

'Little and often' is the mantra one must always bear in mind when rearing young animals suffering from starvation and hypothermia. So throughout the rest of the day Julie fed the otter hourly. By afternoon I returned to the house to discover the otter drinking milk at a healthy rate.

Fortunately, at the last committee meeting, the RSPCA had agreed to offer their support to us, including building a new cattery. It didn't take me long to find out how useful it was to have them on our side. With the otter seemingly out of immediate danger, I rang Ralph Gardner's wife, Jean, to ask whether she could put us in contact with someone at the RSPCA who knew a bit about otters. She gave me a number for Colin Seddon, manager of the RSPCA's wildlife centre near Taunton. I called him immediately.

Colin was helpful. Although he had no experience himself, he knew of a centre in Scotland that would almost certainly be able to give us the information we would need.

The person I then called was Mr Green, who was in Scotland. He was enormously helpful and I was soon scribbling down all sorts of advice.

Thank goodness for the RSPCA, I thought to myself.

In the three weeks or so he'd been with us, the otter had migrated from the Aga to a comfortable box in a corner of the kitchen. Under Julie's watchful eye, he was making great progress and was barely recognisable as the shivering, sodden ball of fur that I'd rescued from the river.

As his strength had grown, so too had his confidence. He had left the safety of his box and was happily wandering around the kitchen, interacting with us. The otter was particularly fond of Julie. Every day he would rub up against her arms and legs, clearly angling to be picked up. He had become friendly with the other animals too. By now our cats and dogs were so used to strange creatures living in their midst they barely gave them a second look. The otter had clearly taken notice of them, however. On more than one occasion, he rolled himself up into a ball alongside the dogs sleeping next to the Aga.

At times it was as if he wanted to be a dog. Sometimes he would roll on his back and chase his tail just like a puppy. At others he would hide inside my gumboots. He had become particularly attached to a long cardboard tube, which he would dive into, then emerge from with his head poking out, chittering away with obvious enjoyment. He was a fun addition to the family. His progress, however, presented us with a new problem.

He was still drinking Julie's mixture of Lactol and fish. In fact, he was so fond of the stuff he would have guzzled it down all day long given half a chance. We knew, though, that he couldn't continue on this diet. He would need to be weaned on to solids, probably fish. Again, the Greens were helpful. They explained that we should be feeding the otter white fish. The meat should be scraped off the bones and we would have to make quite sure it contained no bones. This we did, and the otter was soon switching to this new, improved diet.

It was during one of my frequent chats with Mr Green that we made the decision it was time for the otter to leave us. For some reason Mr Green was under the impression that we were a much bigger sanctuary than we actually were. He seemed to have assumed that we had more than one otter. When I revealed he was the only one we had, Mr Green let out a quiet 'Hmmmmm'.

'You should really raise otters in pairs, Mr Harper,' he said. 'A cub that's raised on its own can easily be humanised. When you release it into the wild it is going to struggle. An adult male otter could easily kill it if it strayed into its territory.'

'Oh, dear,' I said, slightly alarmed by this. Knowing how the otter was behaving around us in the kitchen, I wondered whether he had already gone too far down the road to domestication. 'What should I do?'

'Well, it sounds like you're doing a great job. And it's still early days,' he said. 'I'll see if I can find somewhere near you where it might be able to join some other otters.'

It was a couple of days before Mr Green got back to me. As it turned out, he hadn't been able to find a sanctuary or animal home with another otter in England.

'It looks like we'll have to get him up here to Scotland,' he said.

It was with some sadness that we said goodbye to the otter. Our month or so in his company had been memorable, but we knew that he could not be a domestic pet and that he had to return to the wild. First, he had to learn to be a proper otter. And he could only do that in the company of other otters. I had no doubt he would do that up in Scotland.

We stayed in contact with the Greens and were delighted to hear of the otter's progress. He settled down with a female, and eventually the pair were released into the wild, where they were tagged so that they could be monitored. To everyone's delight, they prospered, raising a family of their own.

The otter was a memorable case for a couple of reasons. I'd learned a lot from caring for him, not least that sometimes you have to improvise, as Julie had done with the Aga. I'd also learned to give the public a little more credit from time to time. Most of all, however, I'd learned how much of an asset it was to have a relationship with the RSPCA. It certainly made me feel less like I was on my own. Deep down, it made me wonder something else as well. For the first time, I wondered whether – one day – I might devote myself to this full-time.

CHAPTER NINE
Permanent Staff

There were times when I wondered how we crammed everyone into the Rosery.

Our fourth child and second daughter, Zoë, had arrived that spring, 1967, ten weeks premature and, at two pounds fourteen ounces, weighing little more than a couple of bags of sugar. But she'd quickly grown into a healthy, happy baby whose cries filled the house.

It was the dogs that had really taken over the place, however. I'd arrive home most evenings to find four sleeping dogs stretched out across the kitchen floor. As I carefully picked my way over their snoozing bodies, I'd shake my head in puzzlement that we'd somehow accumulated so many homeless creatures. 'The sooner we start looking for homes for you lot, the better,' I'd mutter.

Ordinarily, we only ever had one or two dogs at most. In contrast to the cats now residing in the new cattery the RSPCA had delivered to us, it was relatively easy to find a home for a good, healthy, well-adjusted dog. The strays that came to us were regularly rehomed within weeks.

Two things had conspired to swell the canine ranks, however. First, Julie had started breeding Yorkshire terriers. A brand-new litter of four had arrived only days earlier and had been installed in the kennel outside. The dog population had also been increased by two new arrivals, a large Labrador called Cleo and a black poodle called Patti. My intention was that both dogs' stays with us would be as short-lived as possible. Already, however, I had my suspicions neither would be going anywhere in a hurry.

Cleo and Patti were very different dogs physically and temperamentally, but they had arrived with us in similar circumstances. One of the most common calls we were now receiving concerned dogs whose owners were no longer able to look after them. Both had come to the Rosery in this way.

The call I'd received about Patti had come from a policeman. He'd given me the address of a house a couple of miles away, where I had discovered a trio of police vehicles and an ambulance in attendance. Inside the cottage, I had found a police officer and a pair of medics attending to an elderly lady. An oxygen mask had been attached to her face and she was being prepared for transfer to the ambulance on a trolley.

The policeman had then told me the lady had had a suspected stroke and had been lying there for two or three days. A neighbour had alerted the police after hearing a dog bark and failing to get a reply to their knocks at the door. The police had been forced to break the door down to gain entry.

It seemed they had arrived just in the nick of time. The frail-looking lady, probably in her late seventies, was alive, but only just. It had been icily cold and she was now suffering from the early stages of hypothermia, one of the medics told me. 'If it hadn't been for this little lady, I don't think she'd be with us still,' he had added, nodding in the direction of the small poodle that was sitting on the chair looking anxiously at the figure of its owner being readied for the ambulance. 'I think her name's Patti.'

Patti was a little black-coated toy poodle and couldn't have been more than ten weeks old. The medic told me she had been found nestling on the lady's chest. The warmth she'd provided may very well have been the difference between life and death. The attending officers had found no relatives or close friends to care for the puppy, which was why they'd called me. She'd settled down at the Rosery quickly, which was more than could be said for our other new canine guest.

It was another phone call a few weeks later that had brought Cleo to our door. As it turned out, I knew the dog well. An ageing black Labrador bitch, she belonged to a rather surly old chap who lived on a farm in a nearby village with his wife. I'd known the dog for years, since I'd started delivering mail in the area where she lived. Cleo and another Labrador acted as guard dogs – and very efficient ones too. Their barking was enough to frighten off even the most resolute intruder.

Things had changed at the farm, however. The man's wife had died, leaving him alone with the dogs. He'd sold up the cottage and moved into a flat in the village with just one of the

Labradors, the other one having died. I'd often seen them walking around the village. The dog would always look thoroughly unhappy, tagging along with its owner on shopping trips, walking to heel, but looking dejected and not interested in her surroundings. She had also been reluctant to be touched by strangers, preferring to completely ignore them, even though there had been many who admired her looks and would willingly have befriended her.

As I'd watched her over a period of time, I'd also seen she wasn't getting enough exercise. She had developed rolls of fat round her middle and generally seemed unfit.

She had looked like an old, unhappy and unhealthy dog. So when a local doctor had called me to tell me the dog's owner had been taken ill, I hadn't been entirely surprised. Nor was I unduly shocked by his request that I take his dog in.

I had agreed, of course, but began to regret it the minute I went to collect her. Cleo had clearly bitterly resented my attempts to put a lead on her, and pulled relentlessly as I walked her the two miles back to the Rosery.

In the weeks that had followed their arrival, Cleo and Patti had both set me challenges. When I had carried out a careful medical check of Patti, I found all sorts of problems. Not only did she have external and internal parasites, in the form of fleas and worms, but she also had sarcoptic mange, a really nasty condition that is not easy to cure or control. I discovered that the elderly lady had bought Patti from a disreputable local breeder. It was no surprise, then, that the poodle was so badly maintained. I knew her first weeks with us would be dominated by treating her coat. I began washing her every couple of days and administering treatments on a daily basis.

Cleo's problems ran, if anything, even deeper. She was an intelligent dog, with a beautiful wide head. But she kept her deep, sad eyes turned away from me at all times. Even now, a couple of weeks since arriving here, she remained unresponsive, any attempt to gain her confidence met with indifference. Her food remained untouched, and she refused to lie on her bed, preferring to sit in a corner of the kennel.

She'd already run away. We lived about two miles from her former home, and when she went missing I'd doubted at first that she'd have been able to make the journey to her owner's flat in her current unfit state. But I'd underestimated her. Sure enough, when I arrived at the flat I found Cleo sitting on the doorstep as if waiting for her former owner to arrive home. She didn't take kindly to the sight of me turning up at all. It took a real effort to get a lead on her and bundle her into the car.

Back at the Rosery, she resumed her normal position in the corner, her head held low, her baleful eyes filled with sadness, a completely dejected animal. Truth be told, I'd already begun to have my doubts about whether much could be done for Cleo. She was nine years old and clearly unhappy. I couldn't see anyone adopting her, certainly in her present condition. In fact, her prospects weren't good in the long term either, especially if she wasn't going to place her trust in anyone. Deep down, a part of me feared this was a dog that one day might have to be euthanised.

If I'd learned one thing about animals, though, it was that they could make quite dramatic recoveries. As it turned out, Cleo began hers on a long, stormy Cornish night.

The weather had been worsening all afternoon. Heading back to Perranporth at the end of my round, the northerly gales piling in off the sea had blown me off my bike, forcing me to lean into the wind and push my way back to the sorting office. Heading home, I discovered that the rains further inland had already swollen the stream in the valley in Bolingey, sending me on a long diversion round swamped lanes and across muddy fields to get back to the Rosery safely.

Turning in for the night, there were ominous rumbles of thunder in the direction of the coast. On the radio, the weather forecast predicted even more severe storms overnight.

Sure enough, around midnight I was woken by the sound of thunder claps and the flicker of lightning. Soon afterwards, torrential rain began drumming on the cottage roof. The volume of water was such it quickly filled the gutters to overflowing. I wondered whether the old roof would cope.

As we listened to the tumult outside, Julie and I just managed to pick up a strange howling coming from the outside kennel. It wasn't easy to hear with all the noise from the storm, but clearly there was a very scared dog outside. We knew immediately it was Cleo, who had been put out in the kennel on her own.

'We can't leave her out in this, she's terrified. Let's go and see the poor girl,' Julie said, climbing out of bed. Together we pulled on our mackintoshes and boots and made our way out into the night.

The rain was hammering down so hard it almost pinched the flesh when it hit. The ground was already soggy with water lying inches deep here and there. We found Cleo in a dreadful state. She was petrified and shaking like a jelly, her massive rolls of fat wobbling and trembling uncontrollably.

Her demeanour had changed completely. The distant, uninterested dog we'd known had suddenly become a vulnerable and needy one. The moment Julie crouched down beside her and spoke to her Cleo buried her huge head in her lap. Her howling had stopped and she lay there, twitching her otter-like tail contentedly.

'I think you'd better come indoors with us,' Julie said softly to her. Having dried ourselves and Cleo, the three of us were soon settling down, with the dog on the floor next to our bed. She spent the night there, occasionally raising her head to lay it close to Julie whenever a particularly loud clap of thunder broke.

Next morning she stayed close to Julie and ate a good hearty breakfast. Her attitude to the rest of the house was much better too.

'Looks like she might have turned a corner,' I said to Julie.

'Let's wait and see about that, shall we?' she replied.

Christmas was upon us, and for once there was a real prospect of a relaxing holiday season ahead. The festive period had always been a busy time of year for postmen, mainly because there seemed to be no set procedure as far as our main office in Truro was concerned.

In the run-up to Christmas, mail would arrive at Perranporth throughout the day at irregular intervals often until very late in the evenings, so that by the time it was sorted and delivered we did not get home until nine or ten o'clock. The late finishes, allied to the even earlier morning starts we were asked to make at that time of the year made life rather wearing to say the least, so it was no surprise that by the time Christmas arrived tempers were pretty short.

For many years the straw that usually broke the camel's back was the Christmas-morning delivery. For some unfathomable reason, some people felt that their friends would enjoy receiving mail on the great day itself. As a result we had to turn up at dawn on Christmas Day to pick up bulging postbags. We were lucky if we had completed our delivery before midday. I personally found this completely exhausting. Many a family Christmas had been ruined by me arriving home, collapsing into a chair and sleeping through until late Boxing Day, missing the dinner, the presents and everything else.

Thankfully, however, Christmas Day deliveries had finally been stopped and things had generally become better organised so that everything tailed off by Christmas Eve. But it was still an exhausting time.

It wasn't without its bonuses, of course. People were very generous to their postmen at this time of year. Cups of coffee and mince pies were coming out of our ears by the end of the rounds. And for those who fancied a drop of something stronger, a wee dram was always forthcoming.

For my part, I always left it at a wee dram, then made my excuses and left, but there were others who took maximum advantage of the hospitality on offer. A few years earlier, just before Christmas, we'd had to send out a search party one evening to find one of my colleagues who'd failed to return to the sorting office. We eventually found him sitting in the middle of the road. He said he was trying to 'roll up the white line'. Goodness knows how much he'd had to drink.

The generous Christmas tips we got were welcome too, providing a much-appreciated boost to the family coffers at this most expensive time of the year. These tips weren't always monetary, though. One morning a farmer waved me into his kitchen with a smile. For a moment or two my imagination ran riot and I imagined him handing over a chicken, a goose or even a turkey. My hopes were quickly dashed. Instead he presented me with a large cabbage. 'For Christmas, boy,' he said, with a smile and a slap on my back.

As is so often the case, it was the people with most to give who were the stingiest. One hotelier in Perranporth was notorious for not giving Christmas tips. Then, one Christmas

Eve I dropped the post off at the hotel reception and was told that he wanted to see me in his office. Good grief, I thought to myself, I've hit the jackpot at last!

I went upstairs to find the great man sitting behind his desk. Again, my hopes of being handed a wad of banknotes withered on the vine.

'I wonder if you would be kind enough to deliver these local cards for me on Christmas morning,' he said grandly. 'I forgot to post them.'

I managed to come up with a diplomatic reply, regretfully telling him the Christmas-morning post was no longer in service.

My language was a lot fruitier back in the sorting office, I must admit.

This year, however, Christmas Eve had been a fairly quiet day. After a quick drink with the other chaps I headed home, looking forward to an early night and a nice lie-in on Christmas morning. The children could get as excited as they liked. As I put my head down, I promised myself I wasn't going to budge from my bed until at least eight o'clock.

Fat chance. The sun had barely broken through and the clock was showing just after seven thirty when I heard Julie shouting.

'What is it?' I said, rolling reluctantly out of bed.

I looked down the stairs to see Julie standing in a foot of water.

'Looks like we've had a flood,' she said, as she tried to take stock of things. After a moment or two a look of panic crossed her face. 'Oh, no, the Yorkies,' she said.

Julie was still breeding Yorkshire terriers and three of them were in the living room.

We both sloshed our way through the rising water towards

the front of the cottage. Julie need not have worried, however. As we opened the door to the living room we saw the most remarkable sight. There, lying in the middle of the room, was Cleo. Lying on her back were the three Yorkies, all fast asleep, oblivious to all that was going on around them.

Since that stormy night a few weeks back, Cleo had become a different dog entirely. She had remained devoted to Julie, who had placed her on a rigid diet to reduce her weight. Cleo had also started regular exercise and her muscles had begun to take shape again.

Her owner had left hospital but wasn't well enough to take her back. Each week she would visit him, sometimes accompanying him on a slow walk around the village. She was always delighted to see him. In her owner's company she was her old quiet self, but the moment she got back to the Rosery she was bounding around making a fuss of Julie.

Cleo and Julie were inseparable, but the dog had also formed a real bond with our two girls. On many an occasion Julie had discovered Klair or Zoë fast asleep with their heads resting on the Labrador's warm body. Klair had even taken some of her first tottering steps while holding on to Cleo's back. It was a responsibility the old dog took extremely seriously, and she moved along very slowly and carefully as the toddler picked her way across the floor.

It was a Christmas to remember, if not for all the right reasons. It turned out the leak had come from a pipe in the kitchen. Given the quantity of water, the pipe must have been gushing out for hours. I couldn't work out how we'd not spotted it before going to bed.

There was no use crying over spilled water, though. Instead we spent the day trying to dry out the house. The carpets were completely destroyed so we began by ripping them up, no easy task, as the water made them incredibly heavy.

With the carpets removed, most of the water drained away within a couple of hours, but the house was still damp and musty-smelling. We put the Aga on full blast in the kitchen and lit a wood-burner at the other end of the cottage.

Miraculously, Julie still managed to produce a Christmas meal and we were able to play a few games with the children. But it was far from the quiet Christmas I'd been looking forward to. Quite the opposite in fact.

The following day, Boxing Day, the weather was fine, so in the afternoon we decided to go to the beach. We took Cleo and Patti the poodle with us.

Like Cleo, Patti had very much become part of the family. While Cleo's loyalty lay with Julie, Patti had quickly become my shadow, never leaving my side when I was at home and moping around the house whenever I left for work.

Patti's only weakness was her dislike of water. Poodles were originally water retrievers, but clearly Patti's parents had failed to pass on that part of her genetic inheritance. Whenever we headed to the beach as a family she would stick resolutely to the sand. Nothing we did could entice her into the water, and so it was today.

Instead, as usual, she concentrated on the role that came more naturally to her, guarding our clothes and belongings while we splashed around at the edge of the sea.

Cleo, on the other hand, loved being in the water. Even today, with the water too cold for us to brave, she ran straight in. She then swam around through the surf like a seal, before turning each time a good-sized wave came along, allowing it to carry her back to the beach.

'Good girl,' Julie said, when Cleo finally emerged from the water ready to head home with us.

As we walked back to the car, Julie and Cleo were all over each other again.

'Looks like she's going nowhere for a while, then,' I said.

Julie smiled at me and was quiet for a moment.

'Actually, I've been meaning to have a word with you about that,' she said eventually. 'I was thinking we might keep Cleo as a dog for ourselves.'

I knew I wasn't going to win this argument, nor was I sure I wanted to. But I made my objection nevertheless. 'I thought we'd agreed that we wouldn't hang on to the animals. If we're going to run this place like a proper RSPCA centre, then we can't be so sentimental,' I said.

To be honest, my heart wasn't in the argument, and Julie knew it. 'It's not as if we're going to do it all the time. Just every now and again,' she said. 'Besides,' she added, smiling broadly as if inspiration had suddenly struck, 'look how helpful a good dog can be. If it hadn't been for Cleo, the Yorkies might have drowned in their sleep. We shouldn't look on her so much as a pet, more a permanent member of staff.'

What could I say to that? Not a lot.

By the middle of January Patti had been introduced to her new role as a post dog. Each morning she'd climb into my postbag and head off with me to the sorting office. We'd then set off on our round.

She'd taken to the role like a duck to water. I'd done some basic training with her and she'd learned to accept commands well. She'd also learned to sit and wait. She would walk the round with me, patiently waiting at each gate as I delivered the mail.

Patti enjoyed this immensely and easily kept up with me as I walked the lanes. The only people who didn't seem to approve of her new role in life were my two sons. Clearly they felt their father being seen with a tiny toy dog was embarrassing. I'd often see them on the school bus passing me and could see their scarlet complexions as schoolmates pointed me out. Once, out of devilment, I waved to them with a limp hand and placed my hand on my hip. I don't think they ever forgave me for that!

Patti turned out to be a surprisingly good guard dog. On the round her presence ensured I never had any of the traditional troubles that afflicted postmen up and down the country. If there was a dog present, it would be more interested in Patti than me.

She was also invaluable when I went out in the post van, which had replaced my bicycle. Patti would sit on the passenger seat making sure no one ever got anywhere near the all-important cargo of parcels and letters in the back. Just how determined she was to guard Her Majesty's mail, and me, I was about to discover.

One day we finished the morning round and rather than heading back to the Rosery, we set off for a retirement home on the outskirts of Perranporth. Patti's original owner had made a partial recovery from her stoke but had been forced to move to the home rather than return to her old cottage. The home had been in contact and had asked if Patti could come along to see her. She'd been asking about her dog a lot, apparently. Today was going to mark the first time she'd seen Patti in several months.

The old lady's face lit up the moment she saw her beloved poodle walking into the room. Patti, too, was clearly delighted to see her old companion, wagging her tail and jumping up on her lap at her request. We spent twenty minutes or so with the lady. She wasn't well enough to walk yet, but we promised that – at a future date – we'd take her and Patti out in the grounds so they could take a stroll together.

As I watched the lady and her dog together, I wasn't sure whether this was going to change Patti's attitude towards me.

Perhaps she'd be reminded of her old life and want to go back, not that that was possible, of course.

Any doubts I had about her future were erased the moment we walked back out of the retirement home. Immediately Patti was at my side, looking up as if to say, 'Where are we off to now?' then fussing to get into the van and go back to the sorting office and out on the afternoon round.

That afternoon we went out, as usual, delivering parcels and other items in the area. Whenever I got out of the van Patti would stay inside acting as my lookout. Despite her size, she clearly imagined herself to be my guard dog.

I had just climbed back into the driver's seat after making a delivery in Bolingey when I was approached by a beefy lorry driver, who appeared at the passenger window, asking for directions to a local property. He was a rough-and-ready character. To hear me better, he leaned into the van through the window. As he did so, he saw little Patti, curled up in a defensive-looking ball and looking somewhat apprehensive.

'Suppose that's your bloody guard dog?' he said, unable to suppress a hearty laugh.

The smile soon disappeared from his face.

Patti clearly took exception to the remark and flew at him. Terrified, the poor chap threw up his head and hit it hard on the roof of the van. As he withdrew his head he unleashed a torrent of expletives. Suffice to say, he wasn't best pleased with Patti. I wasted no time in slipping the van into gear and pulling off.

Back home that evening, I told Julie what had happened. She couldn't stop laughing at the idea of a poodle terrorising someone.

'Did you hear that, Cleo?' she said, giving her dog a reassuring ruffle on her neck. 'Patti's got a new job as a guard dog.'

'That's right,' I added, giving my own companion an

affectionate pat and arriving at a decision about her future at the same time.

'Looks like you've joined the permanent staff too, young Patti,' I said, loud enough to ensure Julie heard me. Her face was a picture.

CHAPTER TEN
Pastures New

By the mid-1970s the days when the family could comfortably live together in the Rosery were over. The boys were now in their teens, and the girls were getting ready for secondary school. For the past couple of years we had been fostering more and more children, and one of them, Maggie, seemed to have become a permanent member of the family, as had a sizable number of animals, from Cleo and Patti to our collection of ducks and chickens. When we were all together under one roof, it felt like we were sardines in a tin. Even with the former schoolhouse in the garden now converted into extra accommodation for the family, there simply wasn't enough space for us all.

It's strange how fate can play a hand at times like these. Soon after my fortieth birthday, my mother died at the age of eighty. The inheritance she left me was just about sufficient for a deposit on a larger property. So when Julie and I heard about a smallholding coming up for sale a couple of miles inland from Bolingey, we arranged to view it. We both took one look at the place, on the side of a hill a few miles outside Perranporth, and fell in love with it.

It was called Ferndale and was set in eleven and a half acres of land, made up of several small, gently sloping fields bordered by a disused railway bank, with woodland to the north and a trout stream at the south-east.

My guess was that the land was linked to the local copper industry. The telltale earthworks of two 'capped' mineshafts were visible in the lower fields, and near the fast-flowing stream at the boundary of the land, a ditch carried water that was a deep orange-red in colour. I suspected there had once been open-cast mining and that the ditch had been dug to provide drainage. To judge by the colour of the water, the deposits of iron oxide buried deep beneath the soil were obviously still rich.

The farmhouse itself was around two hundred years old and probably originally belonged to the manager of the mine. Set back off a quiet country road, it was square-built with a scantle slate roof facing south-east. Inside, it had two double bedrooms and one single with a sitting room and living room below. The rear of the house, under a steep, sloping roof, was made up of a good-sized dining room, kitchen and a dairy.

On the downside, the interior of the house was in a pretty rickety state and would need fairly major renovation. There was no proper bathroom, and the loo was outside. But we'd overcome problems like that before at the Rosery and weren't daunted.

From my point of view, the other great asset the place had was its outbuildings, which were ideal for keeping the animals. The couple who currently lived in Ferndale ran a small milking herd. The Rosery's collection of pens and cages were hopelessly overcrowded. Here, there was a conventional Cornish stone barn, with a hayloft upstairs and 'tie-ups' for eight cows below. There was plenty of space for new buildings to be erected too. I could already picture the layout of the sanctuary we would build here. It was perfect.

Our negotiations with the owners proved unconventional. We knew the couple a little already. They'd lived at Ferndale for twenty-three years but were coming up to retirement and were looking to move to a smaller property in Perranporth itself. It was clear, though, that the wife was much keener on the move than her husband. We expressed our interest and asked them to keep us informed.

Weeks went by without a word, but then late one evening we had a knock on the door. The husband and wife were standing there looking a touch embarrassed. We ushered them in and Julie rustled up a cup of tea.

The small talk went on for a few minutes before the wife cleared her throat and announced, 'Well, I've made up my mind, and whether he likes it or not, we are moving.'

Her husband smiled thinly, then fixed his gaze on the floor.

'So,' his wife continued, 'if you're interested, we can talk business.'

It took a few weeks to get things moving, but we eventually exchanged contracts. We put in an application for a council grant to rebuild part of the building and were soon told we'd get a council inspector's report telling us what needed to be done – and more importantly – how much money they'd give us to do it.

A fortnight or so before we were due to become the farm's new owners, the old ones decided to have a sale of all their stock. I went along and was amazed at the amount of farming ephemera spread out across the fields. There was everything from wire netting and corrugated iron to milking equipment and an electricity generator. All of it went under the hammer and all of it sold. I watched, shaking my head in wonder as people staggered away with arms full of various bits of bric-a-brac. I knew the auctioneer to talk to and he came over to me at the end.

'Went well,' I said.

'Yes, cleared the lot. Plenty of bargains out there,' he said, before turning to look at the farmhouse. 'Which is more than can be said for that place.'

'Why do you say that?' I asked.

'Well, put it this way,' he said, 'I reckon any mug that buys that place needs his head read.'

I simply nodded.

On a bright April morning in 1976 we loaded the last of our belongings into the large, open lorry we had hired from a local haulier, rounded up the children, then coaxed Patti and Cleo, a cross-bred boxer called Jess, six Yorkshire terriers, three cats and several parrots into the back of our car.

A collection of other animals had already been dispatched to our new home, packed in an assortment of boxes and cages. There were no tears as we left the Rosery for the last time. We were sad to leave our home of so many years, but deep down we all knew it was time to move on.

The spring weather had been exceptionally good and the sun was shining as our mini convoy pulled up outside Ferndale. We knew we had a lot of work to do inside the house, so we unloaded the furniture and family belongings in the front garden, ready to be sorted over the days ahead. Seeing it all spread out there, it struck me how much junk we'd accumulated. We quickly worked out there wasn't room for anything in the house in its present condition, so we moved a lot of the stuff into the cowshed.

We had already set builders to work inside the house and there were only two habitable rooms. The boys were coming up to their exams and we were worried they might not be able to study, so we'd taken up the offer of a flat in Perranporth where they could stay while we got straightened out. That proved a lengthier process than we could have anticipated.

The council surveyor's report on the farmhouse hadn't made pleasant reading. Indeed it had been something of a horror story. It had turned out that the old house had at some point been struck by lightning. This had resulted in cracks in the end wall, which had allowed rain to steadily seep in over the years. The reading on the damp meter had, apparently, been the maximum level it could reach.

In a similar vein, the joints underneath the wooden floor in the sitting room were rotten and had given way, which meant it had to be entirely relaid. There were other problems too, in particular in the kitchen. The ageing Aga was pronounced unfit for use, and all the electrical wiring was found to be faulty. Even the rather lovely-looking old stone-built chimney was deemed too dangerous. The only good news was that the council had been prepared to give us a full grant for refurbishing the house.

The long, laborious and very messy process of ripping up floors, removing bulging ceilings and loose plaster was well under way when we moved in. Everything we touched, it seemed, was covered with dust and grit. We soon got quite used to having a frosting of cement dust on our clothes and meals. It could be upsetting at times, but we consoled ourselves with the thought that one day we would have a wonderful new home.

Predictably, the old house threw up plenty of surprises. In the sitting room, a tiny fire grate protruded into the room flanked on each side by built-in wooden cupboards. One day, trying to open a sticky cupboard door, I gave an extra hard tug and the whole thing came away. Not only did the cupboard leave the wall, but it took with it a large quantity of loose plaster from over the fireplace, revealing a thick wooden lintel and, with a little more work, a large open fireplace.

The discovery got everyone excited. Soon the whole family were at work removing bricks and plaster and getting themselves covered in soot. The effort was worthwhile as we ended up with a wide fireplace deep enough to walk into and with a 'clome' or pottery oven set into one side wall. We replaced the cracked wooden lintel with a granite one, pointed up all the stonework and installed a wood-burning stove. It transformed the room.

After several weeks working on the house in the evenings and at weekends, we had just about gutted the building. We now needed to get a builder to do the more demanding structural work.

A builder called Archie Pheby and his sons came over from a nearby village. Archie weighed up the house solemnly. The replacement floors, walls and ceilings in the house didn't seem a problem. But when he took a look at the back three rooms under the sloping roof, he began shaking his head slowly.

'Don't go much on this,' he said. 'Better if you took the whole lot down and started from scratch.'

We had no complaints about this. The prospect of new ground-floor rooms appealed enormously. So shortly afterwards, with the council's permission, Archie and his men arrived to start the demolition work.

It proved an easy operation.

'This chimney breast should come out easily,' one of the sons said, raising a large, seven-pound hammer and readying himself to hit the wall above the ancient Aga. He was dead right. He hit the wall once and the whole thing collapsed, making a noise like distant thunder and throwing up an enormous dust cloud. And it wasn't just the wall that fell. Suddenly the chimney came crashing through the roof above us, narrowly missing our heads, then smashing into the pile of rubble that had already accumulated at our feet.

'Well, that was ready to come down, wasn't it,' smiled Archie, as Julie and I stood fixed to the spot, the shock clearly etched on our faces.

As the building work took shape, the house more and more began to resemble a home. Apart, that was, from one corner of the old building. It was to provide the last, and most unsettling, surprise.

Ever since we'd arrived at Ferndale, I'd noticed something odd and oppressive about the atmosphere in the sitting room at the front of the house. It was a dark room, certainly compared with those at the rear of the house, where the sun streamed in all day long. But, to me at least, it felt cold too. Even during summer it seemed like a fridge whenever I went in there.

The feeling that there was something not quite right about the room had deepened in the past few weeks. Frequently when I passed the closed door, I felt as if there was someone inside and that I should look in on them.

At first I'd dismissed the idea, but there had been no shaking it off. Every now and again I'd burst through the door, expecting to see something, but of course there was never anyone there. Just the same strange atmosphere.

I had mixed opinions about ghosts. On the one hand, I

knew there were often perfectly rational explanations for seemingly strange events. When I was in the RAF, for instance, there were a lot of strange stories about a supposedly haunted hangar at RAF Mountbatten in Plymouth. Dogs, in particular, were highly sensitive to the ghostly presence there, or at least that's what people believed until a more prosaic explanation emerged. It turned out the hangar had an electrical system that emitted a high-frequency impulse that was distressing to the dogs' sensitive ears.

Having said this, I did have one experience that I have never been able to explain. Again it was when I was in the RAF. My first dog, Sally, had grown elderly and ill. During one period of leave I returned home to find her very poorly and frail. Her quality of life was rapidly decreasing, I knew, so I made the decision to call in the vet and have her put to sleep.

It was a very emotional moment. Sally had been my constant companion for much of my teenage life and I'd missed her when I'd joined up. She, too, had been very upset when I'd left home, according to my mother. I shed a tear as she left me for good.

A couple of days later I was standing in front of the mirror in my bedroom putting on my tie when I saw Sally's reflection. She was sitting in her normal position at the foot of the bed, just as she had done when I was a young lad. Of course, when I turned round, she was gone.

Given this, then, I had an open mind about what it was that was inhabiting the sitting room. I wasn't going to jump to any conclusions. In truth, I was too busy to think about things too much.

But then, one Sunday, when we were all sitting around the dinner table, I brought the subject up. To my surprise, Julie, the boys and one of the girls admitted they had experienced the same sensations. Somehow sharing our secret seemed to lift the tension we all felt about it. From then on we joked about the sitting-room ghost.

In the weeks that followed, the atmosphere in the room changed dramatically. We put in a new floor and two extra windows, which gave the room a much airier feel. Soon all memory of the ghost had gone – well, almost.

Not long afterwards, I bumped into a farmer who had worked at Ferndale many years back. We got into conversation and I asked him, out of interest, if he knew anything about a ghost or a spirit inhabiting the sitting room. He nodded sagely and went quiet for a while. He then told me how, fifty years or so earlier, a worker on the farm had suffered a serious injury during haymaking. As far as he could remember, the poor chap had been caught up in a threshing machine or some other piece of machinery. His wounds had been terrible and he had been taken to the sitting room of the farmhouse, where, the farmer believed, he had died.

I told Julie the story that evening. We decided to keep it to ourselves.

CHAPTER ELEVEN
'Cheap to Good Home'

For Julie and me, Ferndale offered a chance to broaden our horizons in other ways too.

The idea of self-sufficiency, of a life living independently off the land, had always appealed to us. It had become very fashionable among many people, in part because of the popularity of *The Good Life* on television. Unlike the suburban dreamers who had begun turning their lawns into allotments, however, we had more than enough space available at our new smallholding. We had visions of a small herd of goats, sheep and cows, flocks of chickens and ducks. We saw ourselves producing our own eggs and milk, cheese and vegetables. Who knew, we might even make money out of it, we told ourselves. Things weren't that simple, of course.

Neither of us had a farming background. Julie had an aunt who farmed in Cumbria, and I had a distant relation who was a country vet, but that was about the extent of our agricultural heritage. I had picked up a bit of experience here and there. I knew how to milk a cow and had looked after livestock a little. But I couldn't claim to be anything other than a novice.

Neither of us was put off by our lack of experience, however. We had brought some poultry with us from the cottage, including our pet Muscovy duck, Matilda, and her two daughters. The three ducks took great delight in exploiting the freedom of their new home, taking flights up and down the valley and wandering to the far corners of the land. They began laying their eggs in all kinds of odd places, so Julie and I never quite knew where we'd find the latest batch. Some days they would be in the cowsheds, others they'd be in the dovecote. It made for an interesting guessing game.

The hens, on the other hand, were much more inclined to stay at home, content to forage around the farmyard or bathe themselves in the dust under shrubs. One or two of our bantam hens surprised us by producing broods of chicks, which they'd hatched from eggs they'd incubated secretly in hedges somewhere on the farm. We were soon self-sufficient in eggs at least.

As life began to take shape, Julie suggested one morning that we take our farming efforts to a new level by getting a goat. 'It'll be good practice for getting cows,' she reasoned. 'And we'll be able to milk it in the meantime.'

It seemed a good idea so we scanned the local papers. Sure enough, there was an advert for a nanny goat.

'Cheap to good home,' the ad read.

I hopped on the motorbike and in due course arrived at a rather run-down property with a cluttered backyard. A young lady wearing a long skirt and gypsy-type earrings answered the door.

'Do you still have the goat you advertised in the paper?' I asked.

'Oh, yes, that's Emma,' she said. 'Come and have a look at her.'

She led me through a yard to a meadow where a brown goat was tethered. It was one of the ugliest creatures I'd ever seen. With her dirty brown shaggy coat, a long beard and wicked-looking yellow eyes, she looked terrifying, almost devilish.

'How old is she?' I asked, trying to make conversation.

'Not sure, really,' the lady replied. 'We were given her two years ago, but I don't know where she was before that.'

In my ignorance I had no idea how to age a goat, but I felt sorry for the animal and for her owner, who told me that she had to vacate the property at short notice.

We quickly agreed on a price and sorted out the transport arrangements. Within a couple of days Emma had taken up residence in the cowshed, our first real farm animal.

After a bit of research, I worked out that she was a mixed breed, probably a cross between Toggenburg and Alpine goat, which possibly accounted for her strange appearance. She was certainly no beauty, and those who knew about goats were in little doubt that she was well past her sell-by date. Unlike most goats, Emma was quite content to laze around the farmyard, often standing trancelike with a couple of hens perched on her back, enjoying the sun.

Yet the more we got to know Emma, the more obvious it was that her looks were totally misleading. She turned out to be the most lovable creature. She liked nothing better than being spoken to by me or Julie. When we did so, she would turn her head upside down, squint her devil eyes and smile as only goats can! The children absolutely loved her.

Not long after arriving with us, Emma came into season. After discussing the matter, Julie and I decided to try breeding from her. Motherhood might suit her rather well, we reckoned. We found a partner for her on a farm a couple of miles away.

One morning I walked her along the lanes on a lead and introduced her to her beau. I guessed this was not something new to Emma. The moment she arrived at the neighbouring farmyard gate, she started bleating and wagging her tail like a windmill. She was plainly very keen to get going.

No sooner had I opened the gate than Emma was wrenching the lead out of my hands. Within an instant she'd reached the far corner of the yard where a somewhat surprised but doubtless highly delighted billy goat was tethered. I left them to it.

Encouraged by our first, tentative attempts at rearing livestock, we decided the next logical step would be to get some cattle.

Our first acquisition was Hazel, a two-month-old Guernsey heifer we bought from a smallholding nearby. It was soon apparent that the owners knew even less about livestock than we did. Hazel had been badly reared. She was thin and suffering from a bad bout of scour, or diarrhoea, on arrival.

It would become an all-too-familiar pattern over the years. Before we could get on with the job of farming, we'd first have to perform our more familiar role, bringing animals back to health.

While we nursed Hazel, we were given the chance to acquire an older cow. The two-year-old Jersey, Lucy, was no longer wanted at the farm park where she lived, and we jumped at the chance of moving her into Ferndale. This time, at least we'd be guaranteed some milk, we reasoned.

Lucy arrived one evening in the back of a trailer. She was dark brown with a black face, a friendly nature and an udder full of milk. Everything seemed fine at first, but we were learning that things are seldom as they seem when it came to farming. Sure enough, within hours of her arrival Lucy too began to scour.

At first we assumed this was the result of her journey. Being thrown around in the back of a trailer had affected her. But when the scouring persisted, becoming more and more watery, we got anxious and called in the vet. To our dismay, he diagnosed Johne's disease, a chronic infection affecting the intestines, causing persistent diarrhoea, general weakness and emaciation. The vet thought she'd probably contracted it from the exotic animals she'd lived with at the farm park. He told us that Lucy was very ill and would need lots of indoor rest, with a basic diet of hay.

We couldn't quite believe our bad luck. Somehow, we'd chosen two sickly cows that would need to be nursed back to health before they were going to produce anything for our consumption.

As our first summer at Ferndale wore on, our problems only got worse. The warm spring had turned into a sweltering summer. Every morning the sun rose in a clear blue sky; by midday the heat became oppressive, the whole atmosphere unusually dry, and the evening sunsets a brassy red glow, the sun a brilliant ball of fire sinking slowly into the sea. There had been no significant rain for months and the fields, which should have been sprouting fresh new grass, were an expanse of dried-out brown.

Both Hazel and Lucy were improving, but they needed supplies of hay and grass, neither of which was exactly plentiful. As the drought deepened, Julie had to lead the two cows around the lanes and the road verges to find patches of greenery for them to graze.

By mid-autumn, however, the landscape had changed –

literally. The first welcome rain revived the parched earth. It was too late for the trees, which had given up the struggle and lost their leaves early this year, but at least some grass started to grow and the farm became green once more.

Thankfully, Lucy had, by now, become fit and well and had started producing good quantities of high-quality milk. Seizing her chance at last, Julie had started making cream and butter and quickly found a ready market for her produce among the locals. Encouraged by this, we bought another couple of Jerseys.

Once more, our choices left something to be desired. The latest addition to our bovine family was called Catherine. She was a large Jersey from a milking herd that was being sold up by a local farmer. Adding to her attraction from our point of view, she was in calf and expected to give birth soon. On arrival at the farm we turned her straight out into the autumn fields to await the big day.

The omens weren't good from the beginning. From her first days with us I felt there was something not quite right about this cow. She had a malevolent gleam in her eye when we approached her, and, unlike most Jerseys, she seemed to dislike human company.

My suspicions proved well founded. One evening as I made my rounds of the aviary and cattery, I heard Julie shouting for me. 'Rex, come quickly, Catherine's having trouble delivering her calf.'

I arrived in the top field to see the cow moving around in a very agitated state, blood emerging from her rear end. It was clear she was having difficulty. Julie moved towards her to try to help, but it was plain the cow wanted no assistance. She charged furiously at Julie, almost ramming her with her flailing head. Julie was lucky to get back to the gate enclosing the field in one piece. We made a quick phone call to a neighbour, who had in the past professed himself something of an expert on cattle. He arrived minutes later with a reassuring look on his face. He strode confidently towards the cow, who was by now lying down with a half-born calf protruding from her. She was straining away to no effect and seemed to be exhausted. Seeing someone approaching, however, Catherine summoned up reserves of energy. With a heave she got herself to her feet and chased the would-be midwife out of the field, bellowing at him all the way.

'She's a bugger that one,' he said as he hurdled the gate.

We were getting concerned now. We watched as the cow lay down again and started her futile pushing and straining.

By this point Julie could stand it no longer. Climbing into the field, she quietly crawled through the grass like a commando creeping up on an enemy lookout post. By taking a long, wide arc away from the cow, she was able to crawl round the back of Catherine. After a tense couple of minutes she had arrived in a good position, directly behind the cow and within reach of the calf's legs. For a few moments Julie timed her movements to coincide with Catherine's. As the cow strained so Julie tugged at the calf's legs.

To everyone's immense relief, the calf was soon sliding out. The cow owed Julie a huge debt of thanks, but of course she didn't see it that way. As she turned round to inspect her new-born, Catherine sensed she had company and once more heaved herself up ready to charge. But this time she was too slow. Julie had already started running back towards the gate and safety.

'There,' she said, regaining her breath and looking rightly pleased with herself. 'One calf, safely delivered.'

In time Catherine joined Lucy in the milking barn, where she supplied us with plenty of milk. But she remained an obstinate and aggressive animal. She disliked me in particular and hated having me milk her in the morning.

I was always wary around her. One morning, however, she saw her chance. As I was passing her in the narrow milking stall she suddenly threw her body at me. I was left pinned between her and the concrete wall with my legs trapped. There was no doubt in my mind Catherine was trying to crush me.

Fortunately, she was tied up and was unable to turn her head. I managed to ease myself up on to the rails of the milking stall and heave myself out to safety.

It was the straw that broke the camel's back as far as I was concerned. Catherine was simply too dangerous to be around on a small farm like ours. I made a few phone calls and soon found a dairy farmer who was willing to buy her for rearing calves.

Perhaps she'd been bad luck, I don't know. But Catherine's departure marked a change in our fortunes as far as cattle were concerned. We had soon acquired two more, both of whom were as Jerseys should be: easy to handle and producers of the best of dairy products.

As our first autumn at Ferndale moved into our first winter, Julie and I were settling into a new routine. We would get out of bed at about five thirty each morning and start the milking together before I left for the sorting office.

It was hard work, of course, particularly as I still had the animal patients to care for each morning as well. But I quickly learned to love milking. There was something about getting up in the half-light before dawn, the smell of the hay and the warmth of the cow on the coldest of mornings.

On more than one occasion I looked across at Julie milking the cow next to mine and wondered how the pretty, well-dressed girl I'd married had come to end up sitting on a three-legged stool in overalls with straw in her hair and her face being swished by a cow's tail. One thing I did know, however. She, too, was blissfully happy to be there.

Apart from everything else, the cattle brought a great deal of fun into our lives. Julie and I fairly quickly came to the conclusion that some cows have a rather sadistic sense of humour. A couple of times I'd started milking away in an early-morning trance with the cow chomping happily on her hay and the milk bucket filling nicely, when suddenly I was aware of a muddy hind leg being lifted. Before I knew it the hoof had been plonked directly into the bucket, rendering the entire contents useless. Throughout, the cow pretended to be oblivious, of course. I was expected to believe it was an accident at worst. But if it wasn't premeditated, how was it that the cow always waited until the bucket was full?

Unfortunately for her, it was Julie who was on the receiving end of the most malicious piece of behaviour by one of our cows. She was in the cowshed milking one morning when one of the children arrived with a friend. He was a very polite chap and stepped forward to introduce himself.

Cows are always a little nervous of strangers, and Julie was standing behind the one she had just milked. Realising a stranger was also standing behind her, the cow promptly lifted her tail and shot a stream of extremely liquid dung all over Julie, who was just at the point of turning round to extend her hand to the young man.

'I don't think we had better shake hands, do you?' she said, to howls of laughter all round.

The children had just got in from school when Julie appeared in the kitchen with an excited look on her face. 'Who wants to try our first batch of goat's milk?'

'Me, me, me!' shouted Klair, as she rushed out through the back door. Her sister, Zoë, wasn't far behind.

Emma the goat had finally given birth to a pair of kids.

Our first effort to mate her had come to naught. Despite

being a willing participant, for some reason, perhaps her age, Emma had failed to fall pregnant. A second attempt, however, had brought better results. She had duly delivered a pair of daughters, whom she was now caring for in a barn outside.

When a goat produces kids she goes into full milk-production mode. A goat can produce huge quantities of milk, enough for her offspring and to provide a couple of extra pints on top. So, having been summoned by their mother, the children gathered round, eager to sample the delicious-looking snow-white product.

Klair and Zoë each took a sip, then immediately screwed up their faces in horror. 'It's disgusting!' they both declared, spitting out the milk.

'Don't be ridiculous,' I said, cross at their rejection. 'I'm sure it's lovely, it's just different to the cow's milk you are used to.'

'Go on, then, you taste it, Dad,' said Klair, handing me her cup.

One swig told me they'd been completely accurate in their judgement. It was disgusting. The acid flavour hit the back of my throat in a wave. I felt like vomiting.

Julie was the last one to try the milk and reacted in a similar vein. 'Still, at least the babies seem to like it,' she said, as we left the old goat suckling her two daughters with what I am certain was a smile on her face.

It would be a while before we could cancel the milkman. Self-sufficiency was a long way off yet.

CHAPTER TWELVE
The Trouble With Harry

As the painfully long and laborious process of rebuilding the house had drawn to a close, so too had the work I'd put into getting Ferndale's new animal sanctuary organised.

The RSPCA had again been extremely supportive. Indeed, they'd made it plain from the outset that they saw our move to Ferndale as an opportunity for them as well as us. They saw us as expanding our operation.

Soon after we moved, Julie and I had gone along to a meeting of the mid-Cornwall branch, where we'd been introduced to the committee. The people we met there were generous in their praise for what we'd achieved at the Rosery and seemed keen to help us do even more at Ferndale.

The four main members, Roy Stephens, Pat Fogarty, Eddie Merrifield and, of course, Ralph, discussed the possibility of opening an official RSPCA animal unit there. In an ideal world, they told me, they'd like to build a specialist oiled-bird cleaning unit, a cattery and an office building. But funds were scarce so, for now, they could only see their way to buying and installing a large shed, or field shelter, which I would be able to modify to accommodate various cages for a small number of cats and dogs.

To me, this was still wonderful news. On top of the aviaries and flights that I had built myself, this meant we had the makings of a respectable-sized animal centre. We would be the first rescue centre of our kind in all of Cornwall. I was very excited, if a little daunted, by the faith they'd placed in me and Julie.

Life at the farm ensured I never had long to dwell on it, however. Arriving home from the morning postal round one day, I found an RSPCA van in the drive. There was no sign of anyone – or anything – in the van, so I made my way to the field shelter, which had by then been erected at the rear of the farmhouse. It was there that I discovered a uniformed RSPCA inspector waiting for me. He had a cage, inside which I could make out the shape of a four-legged creature of some kind.

'Morning, Rex. Not sure what to do with this one,' the inspector said. 'In fact I'm not sure what he is, to be honest.'

'What do you mean?' I asked, a little puzzled.

'Take a look for yourself,' he said, gesturing towards the cage. 'It's obviously a dog of some description, but God knows what breed.'

The dog, whatever it was, was certainly extremely frightened. When I approached the cage, it withdrew noisily to the back and huddled there, his bright-yellow eyes glowing in the shadows, full of fear.

'Goodness me, he is not a happy boy. What's the story?' I asked.

'He's been causing problems over in Saltash,' the inspector said. He went on to tell me that reports of a strange-looking dog roaming around the town on the banks of the river Tamar had been coming in for weeks. Many of the calls had talked of a curious creature, half-fox, half-dog. Someone had called in and described it as a yellow collie-like dog with a bushy tail.

At first the calls offered concern for the dog. He had been very playful and had been found in gardens playing with children's toys on a couple of occasions. He seemed no threat; in fact, if he was approached, he ran away. His behaviour changed, however, and the complaints had taken on a darker tone. The dog had taken to ripping up the clothes on people's washing lines, which understandably didn't go down well. The locals didn't like it and wanted the RSPCA to take action. The inspector had done just that, setting up a cage trap into which – after much planning – he had managed to lure the troublesome dog.

'Leave him with me,' I said, when the inspector had finished his explanation. 'He's obviously very agitated now. We'll give him some time to settle down, then decide what to do with him.'

I left Harry, as he had been christened by the inspector, in the trap for a couple of hours, hoping he might calm down a little. I gave him some food and water, and began talking to him quietly and calmly. As I did so, I saw he was an oddity indeed.

He was bright orange in colour and resembled a dingo, the wild dog of Australia. I knew of two dingoes kept as semi-tame pets in another part of Cornwall at that time but had not heard of any puppies being bred from them. In all honesty I doubted many people would want such a dog. Dingoes were not known for settling into domestic life or making reliable pets. He was such an unusual-looking canine that I could never be sure, but my guess was that Harry was a cross between a dingo and another breed.

That evening I found Harry curled up in his cage, which I'd kept inside the field shelter. There was enough room there for him to sleep so I left him overnight.

When I fed him before heading to work the next morning, he still seemed nervous. I must admit I spent much of my round that day pondering what to do about our distressed dingo.

Back at Ferndale at the end of the morning round, I decided firstly to get him out of his trap. I shut the doors of the field shelter, quietly opened the wire cage, then sat back and waited to see how he'd react.

Harry emerged slowly, gingerly looking around, then moving about the shelter with his belly flat on the ground. It was only when he'd checked the entire shelter that he made eye contact with me. Despite his timidity, I was pleased to see that some of the fear of the previous day had gone.

I decided to get on with the daily chores inside the shelter, ignoring Harry as I cleaned out the cages and attended to the various inmates and their problems. As I did so, Harry began sniffing at the back of my leg. This was a good development and I rewarded him for it with a 'Good lad.' I then carried on talking to him, softly and reassuringly.

After a while I sat down on a box and stretched out my hand towards him. He was only a couple of feet away but he didn't flinch. I touched his flank for a moment. He let my hand rest there for a second or two, then moved away calmly, so that he was just out of my range. That's a start, I told myself.

When I put a dish of meat in one of the dog pens, Harry happily moved towards it. As he tucked into his meal I closed the door of the pen behind him. It didn't seem to bother him.

Encouraged by this, I decided to take things a step further. Over the following days I began bonding with him with a view to training him a little. I began by letting myself into Harry's pen and sitting on the floor talking to him. When I reached out to touch him, he didn't shrink away. Instead he remained still, his face a blank, emotionless canvas. From there, I began patting my leg and calling him to me. He didn't come with a wagging tail, as most dogs do, but Harry came over and leaned against my leg.

With things moving in a positive direction, I then progressed to putting a collar and lead on him. I knew this was going to be tricky. As an essentially wild dog, I was fairly certain he would never have experienced wearing anything, so I took him in an enclosed paddock where I could, at least, be sure he wouldn't escape. To my delight, the bond I'd built up was such that Harry let me put the collar on him with ease.

Over the days and weeks that followed he responded amazingly well to everything I asked of him, coming to heel, sitting and returning to me with only the lightest of commands. It had been a very long time since I'd worked with such a responsive dog.

Forming a bond with a dog is a wonderful experience, especially when the canine in question has been rescued from an unfortunate situation elsewhere. But it can also bring problems, especially when you get too attached. I kept telling myself I simply couldn't hold on to every dog that took a shine to me or vice versa. Hard as it was, I had to stop myself forging too close a friendship with Harry.

The pack of canines we had at Ferndale had changed recently. Sadly, Cleo had died after a short illness. But thanks to a couple of German shepherds I'd taken in for training, we were still above our quota of permanent dogs, so reluctantly I had to prepare Harry to be rehomed.

We were already getting even more visitors than we'd received at the Rosery. Word of our new, expanded sanctuary seemed to have spread. One morning, less than a month after Harry had arrived with us, a family called to see if we had any dogs in need of a home. They lived on the coast at Porthtowan and had recently lost their family pet through old age. They seemed highly experienced dog owners so I introduced them to the dog lying across my feet. 'Say hello to Harry,' I said.

In the few weeks he'd been with us Harry had made remarkable strides. In many ways he'd surprised me. But I knew his background and could tell he was not going to be easy. I explained how Harry had come to be at Ferndale and emphasised the problems they might face if they chose to adopt him. I suggested that he should be kept indoors for at least twenty-four hours and be exercised on a lead in the garden for a week or so after that. 'Remember, there's a large part of Harry that's wild,' I said.

We agreed that the family should take him for a trial period of two weeks. At the end of the fortnight we would talk, see how he had settled down and make a decision on his future.

I must confess I watched Harry being led off by his new keepers with a fair degree of trepidation. There was something within me that felt it wasn't quite right. At the same time I had a responsibility to rehome our animals. We had to try.

My instincts unfortunately proved correct. The following morning I got a phone call from the family. They had stuck to my instructions and kept Harry indoors for the first few hours of his stay with them. But when someone had called to visit them that evening, Harry had spotted the open front door and bounded straight through it. The family had run after him but were only able to watch as Harry leaped over their garden wall and vanished into the adjoining fields. I was annoyed, not so much with the family as with myself. Perhaps I'd rehomed Harry too soon.

Immediately after I'd finished work that afternoon I drove over to Porthtowan and began searching the area, calling out Harry's name. It was no good. I drew a blank.

I returned every day for four days – without success. On the fifth day I got up earlier than usual and once again drove over to Porthtowan. It was around 5 a.m. Driving along a lane, I saw a familiar bright-orange figure in the morning gloom. He was trotting along the road in the direction of Ferndale, presumably heading home to me.

The moment he heard the car, however, Harry bolted. He went through a gate and ran into a wooded field. He was about to disappear into a copse when I clambered over the gate and called out his name. His response was instantaneous. He stopped dead in his tracks, turned his head and, seeing me standing on the gate, came belting back across the field. The welcome he gave me could not have been more ecstatic. I have to admit, I felt almost as elated to be reunited with Harry myself.

As we drove back home, however, I realised that I would not be able to let Harry be rehomed for some time, perhaps not ever. It looked as if he was here to stay.

In the weeks that followed, Harry became more and more of a problem. He was as good as gold in my company, but he simply couldn't get on with the other dogs at Ferndale. On several occasions I'd had to separate him from the German shepherds.

They – like Harry – were classic alpha-male dogs. I knew it

was a matter of time before they would decide which of them was the top dog, and that one or more of them was going to get badly hurt in the process. I decided to try and find Harry yet another home.

The family from Porthtowan had since returned to Ferndale and taken in another, slightly less challenging dog, so I couldn't place Harry there again. I had, however, recently been contacted by a couple of experienced dog owners living over in the fishing village of Padstow, some fifteen miles away along the north coast. They said they were willing to take on a rescue dog and, when I called them, agreed to take in Harry.

As wise old heads when it came to dogs, the couple consented to a slower, more careful approach to his rehoming. They visited the farm on two or three occasions, getting to know Harry and taking him for walks on a lead. He got on well with them, showing no signs of wanting to break away.

Happy at the progress they'd made, I agreed to their taking Harry home with them. As I'd done with the previous family, I gave them detailed instructions on how to settle him down and feed him, telling them everything I felt they needed to know in order to deal with this very challenging dog.

They left us halfway through a mid-week afternoon. By evening I had received the call I most dreaded. On arriving home, the couple had given Harry the run of the house, making sure the doors were locked and all the windows closed. All, that is, apart from one tiny window high up in the toilet, which they had overlooked and which Harry had somehow managed to scramble through after jumping six feet up the wall to reach it.

This time the vanishing act lasted for over a week. Eventually I got a phone call from the owners of Prideaux Place, a manor house with extensive grounds in Padstow itself.

A manager there told me that a dog answering Harry's rather distinctive description had taken up residence in their deer park.

The call concerned me deeply. There were now real worries about the safety of the fallow deer. Prideaux Place's game-keeper would have been perfectly within his rights to shoot Harry if he caught him harassing his animals. The thing that bothered me most, however, was that I was completely snowed under with work at the farm and the sorting office. I simply didn't have the time to head over to Padstow.

The RSPCA inspector dispatched to the park in my place had no joy in finding Harry, nor indeed did Julie, who agreed to head over there one morning. After a few days I was finally able to engineer some free time and race over to Padstow with the dog trap loaded in the back of my car.

It was late on a summer's evening when I arrived at the big manor house. I set up the trap near some woodland by the main drive. It was a beautiful evening and I sat down on a turreted wall bordering the property and, for a few moments at least, took in the vista of the park with its great trees and its deer grazing peacefully. It was a scene of wonderful tranquillity, but it didn't last long.

Suddenly a movement in the bushes on the other side of the drive a hundred yards away caught my eye. There was Harry, his nose in the air scenting the piece of meat I'd suspended in the trap. I kept quiet, waiting to see what he would do. He started moving towards the trap but then stopped abruptly. His ears dropped back and he tilted his head in my direction. His powerful sense of smell must have picked up my scent.

As had happened last time I'd found him, he bounded towards me. This time he leaped on to me, catching me off balance so that I very nearly fell back over the wall. His joy was unconfined, it seemed. Dingoes rarely bark but he was barking. Harry was normally aloof but he was dancing around and whining with pleasure. It was quite a reunion.

I didn't need the trap. Harry willingly followed me, pressing his body against mine as we walked, and jumped excitedly into the back of the car.

Once more, I felt a terrible mixture of feelings. On the one hand, I had become extremely fond of this eccentric, rather lonely but deep down very lovable character. On the other, it was now apparent that rehoming him was going to be well nigh impossible. I really didn't know what to do.

Harry remained with us through the autumn, but matters only got more confused and difficult. He became overprotective of me and would refuse to allow other dogs near me. Once or twice I caught him eyeing visitors to the farm with a menacing look. A strict word would quickly put him in his place, but I knew I wouldn't always be there to deliver it.

Then, one day, the inevitable happened. A neighbour's teenage son was visiting one of my boys. As he walked across the yard Harry attacked him, leaping at his back and tearing his shirt. Luckily, he didn't do any real damage, but the lad was understandably shaken. From then on I kept an even closer eye on Harry, but again I knew I couldn't be there every minute of every day.

One evening a friend of Julie's came to visit. Rather than knocking at the front door, for some reason she opened the yard gate and headed towards the back entrance. She was immediately confronted by a snarling Harry. He grabbed her by the arm and bit her several times before she managed to pull herself free. The cuts and bruises she sustained were bad enough for her to have to visit the doctor's surgery that night.

She was extremely understanding about the whole affair. Indeed she apologised for venturing into the yard when she shouldn't have. I was mortified, however. I now knew the list of options available to me was very short indeed.

Given what had happened, Harry's chances of ever finding a compatible home had disappeared. Even if he remained with me, he would have to be confined to either a secure kennel or a chain. He couldn't be trusted to run free when there were people – and children in particular – walking around the farm. I simply couldn't risk it.

What made the decision so difficult was the fact that he was such a concerned and devoted companion. He was responsive to whatever training I introduced and was, most of all, an individual animal, a character unlike any I'd encountered before. But the simple truth was, I didn't have the time to devote to him. My priorities were my job, my family and the rest of the animals entrusted to my care.

Hard as I tried to push it to the back of my mind, the awful reality of what I had to do had become inescapable. I sat down with Julie one evening and talked it through. We were in a fairly emotional state, but we both agreed.

So it was that a day later I drove with Harry to the vet. Harry knew nothing of what was happening. He sat by my side as a quick injection was administered. Before the needle left his body he was gone, and I was alone.

I was friendly with the vet and he was sympathetic. But I was too choked up to speak, and drove away to the peace and tranquillity of the cliffs, where I simply sat in the van, looking out over the sea, going over and over the whole saga of Harry, trying to work out why he had been the way he was.

If he had been part dingo, then that might be something of the explanation. His solitary nature, his reaction to other dogs and his eventual aggression pointed – perhaps – to a wild ancestor. The truth was, no one knew how he had come to be in Saltash in the first place. And now we never would.

What I did know, however, was that Harry had left a lasting impression on me, perhaps more than any other dog I'd had in my life, even Sally, Ripper and Patti. Some would say, 'Well, he was only a dog,' but those people would never understand what it is like to bond with an animal in that way.

I'll never come across another dog like that, I said to myself on the way home, the tears still streaming. And I never have.

CHAPTER THIRTEEN

The Bird Calendar

Ever since we'd taken in our first animal casualties back at the Rosery, birds had been by far the most numerous of our patients. Literally hundreds had passed through our aviaries and bird hospital. They had outnumbered our other inmates by a factor of ten to one, at least. They were our most common casualties again at Ferndale, where the cages and aviary now played host to a bewildering range of winged creatures, from blackbirds to bitterns, guillemots to geese.

What I'd come to notice more and more was how seasonal the different species were. Each year was now conforming to the same pattern. The onset of spring marked the start of our busiest time of the year, in terms of sheer numbers of birds. It was then that we'd begin to get the fledglings, the young birds who, for whatever reason, were struggling to make it in the world.

The first were usually young blackbirds who would turn up sometimes as early as March, often the victims of attacks by cats or other birds who had raided their nests. These would be closely followed by thrushes, mostly song thrushes but sometimes the larger mistle thrushes. From April onwards we could expect all kinds of bird species, from robins and sparrows to finches and starlings.

Rearing a fledgling, particularly a very young one, was time-consuming work. I would keep the really young birds – those that hadn't feathered yet – in small plastic margarine tubs lined with kitchen roll and placed inside a thermostatically controlled hot cage.

Many of the species that came our way would need feeding every half an hour, which placed huge demands on both Julie and me. The food they'd eat would vary according to the type of bird. Fledgling blackbirds, for instance, enjoy a mixture of hard-boiled eggs and rich-tea biscuits, mashed up with a fork and formed into small pellets. Given the delicacy of their young digestive systems, each pellet would need to be washed down with water, dispensed via a pipette or hypodermic syringe.

Later, as the birds grew feathers and developed physically, the fledglings would be transferred to a cage, where their diet would be boosted by mealworms.

The key thing with all wild birds, however, was to ensure they didn't become humanised in any way. To allow them to do so would be to ensure their chances of survival on returning to the wild were almost nonexistent.

I'd learned the perils of humanising birds the hard way. When I was a teenager I'd raised a woodpigeon called Charlie. He became so used to my company he would sit on my hand

and even follow me around in the house. I eventually saw that Charlie was a female and that she clearly thought I was her mate. This was all very flattering for me, but must have been incredibly frustrating for Charlie, who kept carrying bits of twig around in the hope she could entice me to make a nest with her.

One day I discovered Charlie had vanished. No one seemed to know what had happened to her, but then I spoke to a neighbour who said she'd heard the sound of gunshots that afternoon. I guessed a shooting party had been nearby and that Charlie – trusting the sound of human voices – had been drawn to them, with predictable results.

She taught me a lesson I have never forgotten, so our fledglings were always kept at arm's length and never spoken to when handled and fed.

Once the young birds were happy feeding by themselves, we began the next phase of the rearing process. The birds would be transferred to a large outdoor aviary where they could develop their flying technique. They would also share the aviary with older birds from whom they would hopefully learn a little about life in the wild. The way the older birds reacted to the sight of cats or birds of prey, for instance, was important in teaching the young birds to fear predators.

This phase of the fledgling's development would usually last around two weeks. At the end of that fortnight, provided there were no setbacks of course, they would be allowed to fly out of a small trapdoor set high up in their aviary to explore the environment outside.

Sometimes birds would leave the aviary and never be seen again; more often, the youngsters would return to the safety of the cage, sometimes for several days. But eventually all the birds would spread out around the local fields and woods and become self-sufficient.

I had always found it hugely rewarding to rear a brood of young birds, then see them released safely into the wild. I once reared a family of pied wagtails from a very early age. I'd been delighted when, having safely steered them through their fledgling period and back into the wild, I met them several times during my postal round. The way in which they greeted me with happy chirps left me in no doubt they recognised their former keeper.

As the weather improved and we headed towards summer, mallard ducklings were another regular arrival. The ducklings tended to get picked off or separated from their mothers by predators like gulls and magpies en route to the water after hatching.

They weren't difficult to rear. If they were very young, they would start off in an indoor pen under an infrared lamp for a few days. It was important to keep them dry at this stage as without their mother's waterproof feathers to protect them, they would be susceptible to chilling if they swam or bathed. For this reason, I made sure the ducks drank water from little containers too small for them to get into when their natural urge to splash around took hold.

Once the ducklings had started to produce feathers, they would be moved into a large grassed compound with a pond, where they would remain until they were fully fledged. At that point I would release them on to one of the local lakes and ponds where there would be no shortage of humans ready to feed them.

Young woodpigeons and collared doves were other frequent visitors during spring and summer. While the former didn't hang around for long and joined up with the many other pigeons in the nearby fields and woods, the doves would often stay with us for several weeks.

The most fascinating bird to come to us was undoubtedly

the swift, which arrived in small numbers each year, usually in late spring. To me, there is something magical about these birds, which spend almost their entire lives feeding, sleeping and even mating on the wing, only visiting the surface of the earth for a few short weeks during the breeding season. Whenever I held a swift in my hand, I was lost in admiration for the dark, deep-set eyes, its hard, tightly held plumage and short tail. Most of all I admired its wonderful wings, a piece of design so brilliant it can support its owner over thousands of miles of flight. When a swift is at rest, its long flight feathers, or primaries, extend far beyond the bird's body. Equipped with these wings, as well as its tiny hooked beak and enormous gape, its minuscule legs and feet and needle-sharp claws, the swift is a master of the upper air, a creature perfectly adapted to follow its unique lifestyle.

We would only take in a few of these mysterious and – to me – evocative birds each spring, usually young swifts that had fallen from their nests or adults that had been injured or grounded in their very distinctive territorial disputes.

Swifts nest under the roof tiles of tall buildings, squeezing themselves between the top of the wall and the slates. Adults can be highly competitive over these sites and fights are common. As they flail and scream away at their opponents, the swifts use their tiny, sharp claws to cling to the walls, but the fighting can become so intense both birds fall to the ground.

Once there, however, the swift's extremely long wings and short legs make it impossible to take off from a flat surface and they become grounded. This, of course, leaves them extremely vulnerable to predators, so they are lucky to be picked up by humans.

If a swift has emerged from its fall unscathed, it can all end happily. Provided there are no injuries, it can be thrown straight back into the air, always making sure, of course, this is done over a lawn or grass field so that if things go wrong and the bird falls to earth, it is not injured. Once the swift is in the air, it loses no time in opening its sickle wings and dashing off into its own environment. It is quite an amazing and thrilling sight, a minor miracle. I often felt elation at having been able to save one of my favourite birds.

Young swifts are not easy to rear in captivity, but a diet of small mealworms and scraped raw liver usually does the trick. This suits similar birds like swallows and martins as well, although the latter also require pellets of an insectivorous mixture – a blend of dried insects, honey and a crumbly cake-like ingredient – to balance their diet.

The most difficult part of rearing arboreal birds like this comes at release time. Once on their own, the young birds quickly have to learn to feed themselves. In nature, their parents would be around to supplement their intake, but our captive reared birds had no such backup and once released had to depend on their own skill.

To give them the very best chance of making it, we released swifts, swallows and martins early in the morning on fine days, close to a stream or pond where insects were plentiful.

The end of May and the onset of summer brought a new set of challenges, many of them set by young rooks, jackdaws and crows. These members of the crow family would arrive for a variety of reasons. As birds that often nested in chimneys, young jackdaws would regularly be recovered from the grates in the houses below. At other times, whole broods would be rescued when chimneys were cleared out.

All the crow family were, in general, easy birds to rear. On release, many young rooks would join up with the wild flocks that flew over the farm every evening on their way to roost in the wooded valley below.

The most problematic birds tended to be those that members of the public had decided to rear themselves. I received many a young jackdaw that had been treated as a pet and become completely tame.

These birds can become dangerous as they mature. With all their fear of man gone, they happily fly on to people's shoulders and heads and perhaps peck away at ears or spectacles. This is fine for those who are used to birds, but extremely alarming for those who aren't. Children in particular could be terrified by a large black bird suddenly landing on their shoulder. Domesticated birds like this face an almost impossible job in fitting back into the wild, where they would be ill-equipped to integrate with their own kind.

The other common arrivals at this time of the year were herring-gull chicks. In recent times a large proportion of Cornwall's population of herring gulls had moved from the cliffs on the coast to the rooftops of the county's towns. One consequence of this was that the number of orphan gull chicks I was receiving was rising every year. Many of them had fallen from rooftop nests on to the streets or gardens below. The good news, however, was that gull chicks are quite resilient and can look after themselves from very early on, moving around and feeding themselves independently.

I tended to keep the chicks in a large compound with plenty of shelter, where they could grow and develop until they were fully fledged at about the end of July. I would then release them on the perimeter of one of the large caravan sites in the area, where they would be certain to find plenty of food either lying around or handed out by holidaymakers and their children.

The diversity of birdlife in Cornwall never failed to amaze me. Birds of prey of many kinds resided in the county, and a lot of them would end up at my door during the course of the year.

Tawny owls, for instance, were quite common. Youngsters were often found at the base of a tree where they had fallen from their nest cavities. Like other birds of prey, we reared them on dead day-old chicks, which we obtained in quantity from a supplier 'up country'. My daughters expressed their horror at this once. The fact was, they were male chicks, which were of no value to the poultry industry and were consequently put down on hatching. They provided food for any number of captive birds in zoos and private collections alike.

Young tawnies grow quickly. After fledging in their aviaries, they would be released invariably to take up residence in the large ash trees behind the farmhouse, from where they'd emerge every evening to fly back to the aviary to pick up the food we'd left there for them. It would sometimes be several weeks before the young owls were skilled enough at hunting to head off into the local woodland and an independent life.

Visitors to the farm always found the owls a great attraction. Many an overnight guest had found a large-eyed owlet sitting on their bedroom windowsill staring in at the bright light. Some visitors to the centre asked to come back in the evenings specifically to watch the owls' feeding time.

Every now and again I would be brought that now rarest of birds, a barn owl. All too often they arrived with severe injuries sustained in traffic accidents. The problem was that the grass verges that skirted the roads and lanes were the natural habitats of voles and mice. Many an owl had been caught in the slipstream of a car or lorry as it tried to fly off with its prey. Unable to fight the force, the helpless owls had been thrown into the path of another oncoming vehicle and been killed or badly maimed.

We raised young barn owls in the same way we raised the tawnies, but when it came to their release, Ferndale was too small and lacking in food for them to finish their training here, so we had to find farms and country properties with enough land and suitable outbuildings for the owls to spend several weeks learning to fend for themselves as predators.

It was to one such farm that I was called once to deal with a nest of barn owls.

The call came through from a lady who lived in a country cottage next to a dilapidated barn. She had seen a pair of barn owls flying to and away from a large unused grain silo and had, quite rightly, suspected that the pair had their young inside.

Owls incubate their eggs as they are laid, so their chicks vary in size and age. This pair was incubating five owlets of varying sizes. The lady had kept a watchful eye on this remarkable find but had soon discovered one owlet dead outside the barn. She'd then begun to hear an almost constant calling from the other four owlets, which was when she called the RSPCA.

Arriving at the farm, I climbed a ladder to the top of the silo and looked in to discover four owlets cowering in a corner. Fortunately, I had brought some dead day-old chicks with me. When I threw some in, the birds dashed forward and gulped them down hungrily. The young owls were starving, and I suspected that their parents had been killed, maybe when hunting for voles on the grass verges of a main road half a mile or so away.

Surveying the scene, I could see what had happened to their sibling. A couple of feet above them, a corn chute connected the silo to the outside world. The eldest owlet had clearly escaped down this pipe, driven by hunger but only to come to grief.

Our best chance of helping the owlets was to feed them in the silo until they had fledged. They would then be able to follow the route taken by their unfortunate sibling, only in this case we would ensure there was enough food until the young birds had learned to hunt for themselves.

To help the chicks make their escape when they were ready, I found a plank of wood and pushed it into position so that it made a ramp from the floor of the silo to the grain chute. The lady willingly agreed to leave food both inside and outside the silo over the coming days.

To our delight, the four owlets were soon growing into self-sufficient birds, able to fly out from the barn each evening to hunt on the neighbouring farmland. It was a real success story.

If there was such a thing as a quiet period as far as birdlife was concerned, it came during the autumn. Among our regulars at this time of the year, however, were swans.

At the end of September pairs of mute swans would start chasing away their cygnets in readiness for the following year's breeding. Faced with life away from their parents, many of these confused youngsters would end up in all sorts of odd locations. We would take in these strays, feed them up and rest them for a week or so in the swan compound. Ideally you should return a swan to where it came from, but as we had no idea where they had originated, we would rehabilitate them either on swanless lakes where they could grow to adulthood undisturbed or on the river estuaries where herds of swans of all ages lived in non-breeding groups. These were particularly suitable, as here the cygnets would be sure of food from the public.

As winter drew closer, however, things would quieten further still, literally the quiet before the storm. The first hint that another busy period was at hand would be the first sight of gannets, Manx shearwaters and storm petrels blown in by the first of the seasonal gales. Soon afterwards we would start to get oil-soaked birds.

Cornish winters were dominated by the large numbers of oil-soaked birds that were found around the coast, generally between Christmastime and March. At this time of the year the gales would churn up the seabed, releasing all the old oil that had sunk into the sands after being spilled, sometimes accidentally, but too often deliberately, by passing tankers.

As a result, vast slicks of oil would float to the surface, creating a real hazard for diving birds like guillemots, razorbills and gannets. The birds would become coated in the sticky, toxic mess as they came back to the surface after diving for fish.

Birds that were polluted well out to sea had a low chance of recovery. With their feathers glued together and their bodies weighed down, it sometimes took them days to struggle their way to the shore, by which time their attempts to clean themselves would usually have made matters worse, due to the amount of oil that they would have ingested. They would also be exhausted from their efforts and suffering from hypothermia. Many were found dead on the beaches.

Those birds that fell victim to slicks closer to land had a better chance of making it. If they were recovered within half a day or so of being coated by the oil, a good cleaning could often save them.

The oiled birds that were sent our way were cleaned up as best we could manage with water and all sorts of detergents. Without specialist facilities, our success rate at this time wasn't great.

Other storm-blown birds came our way during these winter months. Gannets, petrels and sometimes divers came to us, often simply exhausted by the effort of battling gale-force winds out at sea. Generally all they needed was a couple of days' rest before being released.

The most enjoyable aspect of my life with animals was

undoubtedly the moment when I released these birds back into the wild. The pleasure I got from successfully treating any injured creature, then seeing them return to living a normal life in their natural environment was immeasurable. But this was particularly the case with birds. To see a guillemot or razorbill that days earlier had been smothered in black oil and facing certain death now in good health and flying off to sea always gave me a great sense of achievement.

The locations I chose for releasing birds varied, but there was one place that I returned to again and again. Positioned between two bays, near the picturesque village of St Agnes, this stretch of 200 foot cliffs never ceased to take my breath away.

The cliffs were rich in minerals that lent their face a dazzling range of colours, from bright turquoise to ochre red. In spring and summer they were even more alive with colour, emblazoned by the maritime plants that seemed to grow in every nook and cranny. I never ceased to wonder at the way the pink thrift, white bladder campion and golden dwarf gorse thrived in the cracks, or the manner in which ferns like the spleenwort could flourish in the cliff face's dark and unforgiving-looking caves.

As a beauty spot, I had always regarded it as well nigh perfect, and it was almost as good as a launching spot. The sloping clifftops led gently downward for the first fifty feet, before falling sheer to the sea, and were a natural rock garden, covered with heather and sea pinks, campion and dwarf gorse. At one point, a large flat rock jutted out, creating a natural platform that was perfect for the birds to take off from on release. Not only did it allow them an uninterrupted view of the sea, but the strong updraughts of wind coming up the cliff gave the birds valuable extra buoyancy when they took to the air.

Different birds reacted differently to their freedom.

Guillemots and razorbills would usually be in a hurry to get airborne and within seconds would be up and away, their short wings whirring as they dropped down towards the water, then suddenly changing direction to begin speeding out to sea until one could no longer follow them with the naked eye.

By contrast, gannets would walk to the edge of the rock platform and stand there looking out over the sea, sometimes for as long as ten minutes, before opening their huge wings and gliding away. Once they were airborne, however, there was no stopping them. No matter how stiff the wind, they would head half a mile out to sea before swinging round to the left and heading towards Land's End to the west.

Why they did this, I had no idea, although I suspect birds instinctively follow certain flight paths. What I did know was that their predictability made them a great way to make some pocket money. I'd had several small bets with colleagues as to the direction the gannets would take once out to sea. They never let me down!

The releases were always dramatic in their own way, but one or two have stuck in my mind over the years.

One that I will never forget happened one evening when I was releasing a dozen Manx shearwaters from the top of a very high cliff. Shearwaters have difficulty in taking off from land and the best way to get them airborne is to throw them into the air from a clifftop. The released bird will fold its wings and dive down towards the sea and then, at the last moment before it hits the water, it will open its wings and zoom off over the surface of the sea.

As I released the first shearwater, a male peregrine arrived on the scene and hung on the wind a hundred feet above. The shearwater nose-dived towards the sea with the falcon hard on its tail, and I felt certain that the shearwater's end had come. But then, at the very last second the shearwater altered course and headed out to sea. Just inches above the surface, the peregrine performed one of those spectacular U turns that only such supreme flyers can achieve. It climbed up into the clouds like a rocket until he was just a black speck in the sunset.

As I released the second shearwater, I heard a swoosh of wings and watched as the whole procedure was repeated, with the shearwater making good its escape and the peregrine again performing its amazing acrobatics. The entire sequence was repeated with the ten remaining birds. The shearwaters would have been easy prey for a master of the air like a peregrine so I quickly concluded he was playing.

It was one of the most impressive pieces of flying I'd ever seen, but it was – if anything – surpassed by the display I saw some months later, again at St Agnes. This time I was releasing guillemots, in the early spring.

A pair of peregrines was busy prospecting for a nest site on nearby cliffs. The six guillemots I had just released flew off and landed on the sea quite a long way offshore, bobbing away in line as I watched them through my binoculars.

Suddenly the male peregrine left his mate on the cliff ledge and shot out over the sea, dashing towards the point where the guillemots were swimming. Once there, he flew at the first in line, sending it diving under the water in terror. He then moved along the line of birds, forcing each of them to take cover in the same way. It was like watching a line of wooden ducks disappearing at a fairground shooting alley.

Once all the guillemots had submerged, the peregrine flew on for several yards. But the instant the six birds resurfaced, he turned back and repeated the trick.

It was soon obvious all this was meant to impress his mate, rather than scare the smaller birds. Having had his sport with the guillemots, the peregrine called out to his partner back in the nest, his metallic, rasping voice piercing the air. Satisfied she was watching, he spiralled at tremendous speed up into the blue sky, where for fifteen minutes he went through a display of aerial acrobatics the Red Arrows could only dream of performing. It was one of the most amazing moments I've witnessed in a life watching animals – and birds in particular – in the wild.

Was it any wonder that, particularly after a testing day at work, I was always so pleased to head off to this magical spot?

CHAPTER FOURTEEN

Something Wicked This Way Comes

The young, slightly panic-stricken raven seemed too big for the cardboard box in which he had been transported to Ferndale.

As I lifted the bird out to inspect him properly, his size seemed even more impressive. He was huge, with a large head that looked out of proportion to the rest of his body and an enormous, slightly downward-curving beak. His feathers were a dull black, but he had a bright-red gape and – most striking of all – a pair of intelligent black eyes. Just how intelligent, I could never have guessed.

We had heard about the raven from a local bird garden. They had acquired him from a pair of young boys who had taken him from his nest on the high north Cornwall cliffs and raised him at their home twenty miles away in Penzance.

As I could see all too clearly, he had responded well to the diet and care the boys had given him. He was ten weeks old but looked the size of a much older bird.

The problem was, he had become mischievous and sometimes aggressive, as ravens can be. He had begun stealing shiny items from homes and had flown into a nearby campsite and removed the pegs from several tents. Eventually, he had become such a menace that the boys' parents had asked the bird garden to rehabilitate him. They had immediately called me.

My plan, as with all young wild birds, was to get him back into the wild as soon as he could safely fend for himself. But I knew that getting him to this point could be a lengthy process. Not only do birds have to learn to find their own food, they also have to learn to distinguish predators. This can be difficult when a bird has been reared in captivity, close to humans and with no parents to teach them by example.

One of the most important things when rearing wild birds is to keep them as wild as possible. By that I mean they must not be allowed to become too used to human company. If a bird becomes tame, there is really no chance of it surviving once released.

This particular raven certainly had no fear of people, which wasn't surprising given that it had been brought up from an early age in a human family and treated like a pet. We called him Odin, after the Norse god who had a pair of ravens that he took into battle with him.

Odin wasn't too happy to begin with. We placed him in a large aviary cage, where he proceeded to sulk in a corner, refusing to fly. After a few days – much to his obvious delight – we released him to fly around as he pleased. His people-friendly nature soon shone through. So too did his mischievous streak.

Odin would follow anyone who visited the farm or the centre, much to the alarm of some unsuspecting visitors, who suddenly found themselves being stalked by a huge, rather scary-looking black bird. It wasn't long before Julie, myself and the older children seemed to be engaged in constant rescue missions, either extricating people whose clothes had become ensnared in Odin's sharp black beak or fetching him back from some far-flung outpost of the farm where he had wandered off looking for human company.

With so much going on at the farm, I resolved that, in the short term, the best option was to clip his wings, literally.

Odin had started to moult, shedding his dull black baby feathers and replacing them with the beautiful iridescent plumage of the adult raven. I decided that now was a good time to clip the flight feathers on one of his wings.

I knew the new feathers would shortly replace the juvenile ones that I had cut, and that he would be able to fly again in just a few weeks. But for now this painless procedure stopped Odin from wreaking havoc, straying too far and possibly coming to grief.

It was rare to see a horsebox pulling into our yard, so the sight of an RSPCA Land Rover easing one through the gates caused a predictable reaction. Julie and an excited-looking Klair emerged from the house to join me as the vehicles parked.

The expression on Klair's face quickly faded when the RSPCA inspector lowered the door of the horsebox, however. Like the rest of us, she was horrified at the condition of our latest arrival.

Inside the box lay a small Dartmoor pony, no more than six to eight months old. His eyes were half closed, and his woolly chestnut coat was masking a body so emaciated there were ribs visible. His breathing was shallow and seemed to be inflicting pain with each exhalation. He looked close to death.

'He's in a bad way, Rex,' the inspector confirmed. 'This morning we got a court order and took him from the farm where he lived. We'd normally take him to a centre up country for bigger animals, but to be honest we're not sure he's going to last too long. I've put a call in to a vet. Should be here within a couple of hours, he reckoned.'

I knew the RSPCA nationally had to deal with a constant stream of complaints about the neglect and ill-treatment of horses and ponies, but as the inspector had rightly said, larger animals like horses were generally sent to more specialist RSPCA facilities outside the county. We had the odd one or two, but they were usually en route to one of the bigger centres. This was an unusual situation.

'Right, well, we'd better get him into the barn,' I said.

This proved far easier said than done. The little pony was so weak he was barely able to stand. The inspector and I were able to get him upright, but when we nudged him to walk, the strain of putting one leg in front of the other was almost too much for him.

The inspector, Julie and I placed ourselves either side of his flanks to ensure he didn't topple over. We then had to physically manhandle him the short distance from the horsebox to the barn, where we'd quickly laid out some straw. The pony collapsed into it immediately.

Offered some water and feed, he simply turned his head away and closed his eyes.

When the vet arrived an hour or so later, he took one look at the pony and shook his head mournfully. 'I don't think he's going to last another day,' he said with a grimace. 'What on earth did they do to him? Beggars belief that a young pony could get into this state.'

Despite his grim prognosis, he injected some vitamins and fluids into the pony's bloodstream. His advice to us as he left was to make the pony as warm and comfortable as possible and to try to get him to eat.

'What do ponies eat, Dad? I'll go and get whatever it is they like,' Klair said, a look of concern on her face.

'Grass, fruit, hay, all sorts of things,' I replied.

Klair and Zoë were soon rummaging around in the fields and hedgerows looking for fruit and bits of foliage. They found plenty of tasty morsels – apples and blackberries, leaves and nuts – but the little pony nibbled a few mouthfuls, then sank back into the straw, his interest gone.

We all went to bed that night with heavy hearts. Julie and I expected to get up the next morning to discover the worst.

People could display extreme stupidity in the care of all animals. It wasn't only the ignorant and naïve who were guilty of this widespread abuse, either. Even as late as the late 1960s farmers were still using horses on the land. When a horse was past its working best, some retired their former employee, putting it out to pasture and ensuring it a peaceful retirement. But equally there were many who would simply forget about their animals. The RSPCA were called in on many occasions to deal with old horses that had been left to stand in windy or mud-clogged fields for years without a visit to the farrier.

But to my mind the worst were those who bought horses on a whim. The West Country was home to a number of annual moorland pony sales. These were magnets for soft-hearted people with no knowledge of horses and more money than sense. They would buy two or three semi-wild ponies at ridiculously low prices, then take them home to completely unsuitable accommodation.

In one case, described to me by an RSPCA associate, a horse was kept in the back garden of a council house. Others had been found wandering the roads having escaped from unfenced fields or, worse, abandoned by their new owners a few days after being bought.

As I knew myself, many young girls dreamed of having their own pony or horse. Some parents, to be fair, were willing to do what was necessary to make this happen, finding land to rent or purchase and arranging good stable accommodation and care. But equally there were many for whom it was simply a fad. The moment they experienced the unglamorous reality of feeding, watering and mucking out the stable, their interest cooled. Soon they were on to another fashion, and another horse would be left to suffer.

As I lay awake that night, I wondered which category this pony fitted into.

With some relief, we awoke to discover that he was still hanging on. Bracken, as he had been named by the girls, remained extremely weak, but, with a lot of persuasion, he took in a little more food and water. His condition seemed to improve through the day, and we went to bed the second night a lot more relaxed about his prospects. How wrong we were.

The following morning we found him collapsed in the straw. The autumn air was turning chill, and when I touched Bracken's body he was icy cold.

'Julie, you'd better give me a hand here,' I said, sensing his condition was perilous. 'Let's try and get his circulation moving.'

By then we'd been joined by the boys and Klair. All five of us lifted Bracken up on to his feet. We started rubbing his legs and body with warm towels. He was incapable of supporting his own weight, so throughout we had to lean into him to stop him from keeling over.

After a few minutes Bracken shook himself.

'That's a positive sign,' I said, but no sooner had I spoken than he almost toppled over.

It took three of us to support his weight and keep him upright. We carried on in this way for ten minutes or so. Slowly but surely he began to look brighter. He managed to eat an apple and some hay. Eventually he took a couple of steps by himself without falling over. It seemed to mark a turning point.

Over the next few days his condition improved. The vet hadn't successfully explained what was wrong with Bracken as yet. The slowness of his recovery made me suspect it was more than mere exhaustion. I guessed there was something else wrong with him.

One morning I noticed an odd, rather unpleasant smell around him. He was standing up on his own now, so I could take a good look at him. I slipped under him and looked at the underside of his belly. I drew back some of the thick hair that had accumulated there to see what lay beneath. I found a deep, festering wound that ran right across from one side to the other.

The vet was summoned once more, this time to administer a hefty antibiotic injection.

The discovery of the wound on Bracken's belly marked the end of the pony's major problems. In the days and weeks that followed he made an excellent recovery. He would remain scarred for life, physically and, I suspected, psychologically, but he was eventually found a good home, where he thrived.

When an inspector popped in on another matter, some time after Bracken had left us, we finally learned what had caused the problem. The inspector had been part of the team dispatched to remove Bracken from his previous owners. He told me they had found the pony suspended by a rope across his belly.

Apparently, when Bracken had gone down with an illness of some kind, his owners had been unwilling to face the veterinary costs. Instead they'd tried to treat the pony themselves. Unbelievably, part of their remedy involved placing a thin rope round Bracken's stomach and securing it over a roof beam in the barn to allow him to stand. Unsurprisingly, the rope had quickly cut into the pony's skin. The resulting wound had been left untreated and had turned septic.

Was it any surprise he had declined to the point where he was at death's door the day he was rescued by the RSPCA?

Even though I knew the pony had been given a second chance, the discovery left me seething with almost as much anger as I'd felt when Bracken had first come to us.

'It wasn't the pony that needed stringing up with a rope,' I told the inspector.

On their way back across the fields to the house one morning, the girls saw something alarming in the grass ahead of them. It didn't take long to identify the heap of ruffled black feathers lying lifeless on the ground.

'Oh, no, it's Odin! I think he's dead,' screamed Klair.

The sight that greeted them as they moved closer seemed to confirm their worst fears. Odin's eyes were closed, and his beak was gaping open, inanimate as if it had drawn its last breath.

'Oh, poor Odin,' said Klair, close to tears as she knelt down alongside him.

As she extended her arm to stroke him, the prostrate form suddenly let out a delighted croak and leaped high into the air. He then delivered a beautifully timed pinch on to Klair's bottom.

'Odin, you sneaky monster,' she shrieked. 'I'll never feel sorry for you again.'

Pinching the bottoms of ladies and young girls had become a favourite party piece of our resident raven. The first time it happened I was in the fields when I heard the sound of a female voice yelling. I arrived in the farmyard to see Odin firmly attached to the rear of Julie's jeans. It was hard to work out which were flapping faster, the bird's wings or Julie's arms as she attempted to detach the bird.

Rather unkindly, I began laughing at Julie's discomfort. The smile faded fast, however, when I saw Julie was in fact emerging from the house. She wasn't the victim at all. It was a complete stranger.

My apologies were, understandably, profuse and – to her credit – the young lady was very forgiving, despite being bruised.

Bottom-pinching had clearly appealed to the raven's sense of mischief. As today's episode demonstrated, he would now go to great lengths to engineer a chance to indulge his hobby.

Such strokes of mischievous genius had become almost daily occurrences for Odin. He was clearly a bird of quite exceptional intelligence. His powers of mimicry were superb, for instance, and on countless occasions he had fooled the dogs by giving them orders in my voice. He'd tricked me too, yelling 'Dad' so convincingly I thought it was the children.

He also seemed to be able to memorise comments visitors to the farm made. Once, he was heard to remark with a broad Cornish accent, 'What a bloody great beak that bird's got!'

Nowhere was his cunning put to more telling effect than in the poultry yard. Ravens are very partial to an occasional chick or duckling to supplement their diet, but these are not easily obtained when their mothers are around. They will defend their offspring with beak and claw.

Odin, however, worked out a crafty technique for distracting them. At first the poultry would panic whenever his huge black figure walked among them, but Odin would leave them unmolested. Once the chickens were lulled into a false sense of security, he would put the next phase of his plan into action.

Selecting a tempting piece of bread from his store, Odin would stalk through the various hens, bantams and ducks in the yard, being sure to catch their interest. Once across the yard and into the field, he would make clucking sounds and throw the bread high into the air. He would then hop sideways away from it, leaving it to the poultry.

The mother hens were always on the lookout for food for their broods and almost without fail they would dash to where the bread had fallen, calling to their chicks, who would follow in a long line. Invariably it was the last chick in the line that paid the price.

With a couple of enormous sideways hops and one neck-breaking snap of his vicelike beak, Odin would quickly dispatch the straggler, swallowing it into his throat pouch without the mother hens or the other chicks noticing. It was a brutally effective piece of skulduggery.

Making a nuisance of himself seemed to be Odin's purpose in life. He was a real pest around the house too, regularly removing the putty from the windows and pecking the stuffing from the seats of the boys' motorbikes. None of this did much to endear him to the family, it has to be said.

To be frank, we all hoped that one day Odin would respond to the call of the wild and use his now fully regrown feathers to fly off and join the ravens that flew over the farm two or three times a day en route to the cliffs of the north Cornwall coast.

We had no such luck, however. Every time they passed over, Odin resolutely refused to budge. If they came too close for comfort, he would hide.

We finally realised that he was a hopeless case when he stole a piece of meat from a German shepherd's, Kaiser's, bowl and took it off to the field. A large male raven from the local pair landed close to him and then approached.

For the first time we saw the tables turned. Suddenly it was Odin who was terror-struck. He let out a petrified croak, then scampered for the safety of the barn, leaving the intruder to grab the meat and sail off into the air towards the cliffs with his prize.

We're never going to get rid of him, I thought to myself.

CHAPTER FIFTEEN
'How Do You Sex a Gerbil?'

With the children packed safely off to school and the house empty, I poured a cup of tea, made myself comfortable at the kitchen table, checked my supplies of pencils and notepaper for the umpteenth time, then waited – a tad nervously – for the telephone sitting in front of me to ring.

When Ralph Gardner had asked a couple of months earlier whether I'd like to run the RSPCA's first central communications centre in Cornwall, I'd been taken aback. It all sounded rather grand. The term 'communications centre' conjured up images of a telephone exchange with a spaghetti-like network of cables and more winking lights than a Christmas tree.

'No, I'm afraid it's a bit simpler than that, Rex,' Ralph had chuckled when I'd told him this. 'Just you and a phone and a message pad. That's about as high-tech as we can do for now.'

For as long as anyone could remember, the inspectors' wives had been the first voice people heard when they called the RSPCA. This network of unpaid female volunteers had performed an admirable service, but by the beginning of the 1980s it was felt the organisation needed a more professional, centralised system. Every county in England and Wales was to get a dedicated telephone service, manned by a paid member of staff by day and a duty inspector at night. All calls would come in to one number, with messages relayed to the relevant inspector by the daytime coordinator.

Ralph and the rest of the Cornwall RSPCA hierarchy had been sufficiently pleased with the work I'd done at Ferndale to put my name forward for the job. I have to admit I was flattered. It would give me the chance to retire from my postal round. I'd loved the job enormously, but after almost twenty years travelling the lanes of Perranporth I was growing weary of it. The idea of being able to lie in on winter mornings when the rain was lashing down outside appealed too.

Having said that, the prospect of being the first voice people heard when they called the RSPCA seemed daunting, as did the responsibility of making sure each case was handled correctly and efficiently. I was confident in my knowledge of animals, but dealing with the public, I knew already, was a different matter.

So, as the clock quietly ticked by on my first morning, in October 1980, I was a little anxious. Fortunately, when the phone jumped off its cradle and rang for the first time, the voice on the other end of the line was that of a local inspector whom I knew quite well.

'Morning, Rex,' he said. 'Can I bring a couple of dogs over later on?'

He explained that he'd been involved in removing two bull terriers from some premises on the outskirts of Redruth. The dogs had been used for illegal fighting and the owner was under arrest.

'That's fine. I think I've got some kennel space,' I said.

I was about to make a note to myself to check the kennels later in the morning, but no sooner had I put the phone down than it rang again.

It was a lady, clearly an upper-class one to judge from her clipped cut-glass accent.

'Terribly sorry to bother you,' she began, 'but I wonder whether you might answer a question for me?'

'I'll try my best, madam,' I said, my pencil poised to take notes.

'How do you sex a gerbil?'

'Ah,' I said, the wind suddenly taken out of my sails. 'Just one moment, madam, I'll check.'

This was going to be an interesting new direction in my life, I thought to myself, as I rummaged around for one of the animal reference books I'd placed to one side specifically for challenges such as this.

My first couple of hours on the end of the phone turned out to be a perfect introduction to the days, weeks and months to follow. People rang the RSPCA for all manner of reasons, I quickly discovered. As well as passing on information on gerbils, that morning I offered advice on how to deal with a dog that had turned on its owner, and guided an elderly lady through the pros and cons of whether to have her cat put down. Most importantly of all, I took down the details of a couple of suspected cases of animal abuse.

One gentleman who rang anonymously had seen a farmer

callously thrashing his horse with a rope. Another had heard the plaintive cries of a dog coming from a small cottage in a village not too far from Ferndale. I passed all the details of these calls directly on to the relevant inspectors. In both cases they were able to visit the scenes of the reported crimes that same day.

By lunchtime my head was spinning with the variety of calls that were coming in. As I put the kettle on, however, I was distracted by the sound of very loud barking outside.

'Oh, goodness, the bull terriers – I'd clean forgotten about them,' I said to a bemused-looking Julie, who was arriving in from the fields as I left the house and ran out to the yard.

I found the inspector who'd called earlier struggling with two very large, extremely aggressive dogs. He was trying to hold one at arm's length. To my horror, the other one was fighting with one of our rescued German shepherds, Kaiser. The flailing terrier had him by the throat.

I ran over to the two dogs, locked in combat, and tried to prise open the terrier's jaws so that Kaiser could break free. But the strength of the bull terrier's jaws was quite awesome and his grip on Kaiser's throat was now tightening so that the German shepherd was gasping for air.

I realised drastic action was needed. Somehow I managed to lift both dogs up off the ground. I hauled the pair of them the short distance to a large, wide plastic water butt in the yard, plonked both dogs in and held them under the surface.

Even submerged in the water the terrier was reluctant to loosen his grip. But as bubbles began to rise to the surface he finally relented. The two dogs were soon spluttering and gasping for air, their coats thoroughly soaked. A few moments later the inspector and I had somehow got the bull terriers into an isolated corner of the kennels.

What a morning, I thought to myself, suddenly pining for the relative peace and quiet of my old postal round.

Manning the telephone line on behalf of the RSPCA taught me much. It opened my eyes to a great deal about man's relationship with animals – or the lack of a relationship in many cases.

As the days and weeks passed and I got into the swing of running the communications centre from our kitchen, I was in turns amazed, amused and appalled by the way people treated animals. In particular, I could not get over the way animals were abandoned.

One morning I got a call from the driver of a dustcart. He had been unloading a consignment of rubbish on to the council refuse tip when he happened to spot a white paw protruding from a cardboard box that was tumbling through the air. He managed to stop the hydraulic tipping machine and investigate. He found two half-grown white kittens crammed together in the box. They were, understandably, extremely frightened. After calling me, he dropped them off at the centre, where they were given a complete medical examination and eventually rehomed.

Other creatures were less fortunate. One caller rang in to tell me he'd seen a dog thrown from a moving car in the middle of a busy motorway. The terrified animal had run across the central reservation, dodging vehicles as it went.

On the other side of the road, it had narrowly missed going under the wheels of a giant oil tanker. Somehow it had managed to reach the grass verge and vanished into the undergrowth of a nearby copse. We were never able to find it.

Fielding calls across the county, I was told about all sorts of animals found in lay-bys. Rabbits, guinea pigs, hamsters, mice and even tame rats were discovered in cardboard boxes or carrier bags dumped at the roadside. It was as if people were taking out some kind of retribution on their animals.

On one occasion I got a call from a girl who had spotted a dog tied to a mooring post in the harbour at Portreath. She had tried to reach it but had been beaten by the bogginess of the mudflats.

Fortunately, I got hold of the nearest inspector. The tide was rising. With the help of a rowing boat he retrieved the dog with the water lapping at its neck. A few minutes later and the dog would have been drowned.

In cases like this, the RSPCA would do their utmost to get a conviction. They would publish pictures of the animal in local papers asking for information should the dog or cat be recognised. It proved a successful approach and led to many prosecutions.

Sometimes, however, I was unable to raise an inspector. This meant that, every now and again, it was up to me to deal with an emergency.

One evening a few weeks after I'd started my new job, I got a call from a local farmer. He'd found a dog tied to a field gate near his property.

'He damned near took my hand off when I went up to him,' he said. 'He's scared stiff, I'd say.'

It was blowing a gale and the rain was teeming down so I donned my waterproofs and headed off. I found the dog, a small cream-coloured collie-cross bitch cowering by the gate. She was shivering and obviously extremely upset. I'd learned in situations like this that the direct approach was sometimes the best one. I walked to the dog slowly, giving her some encouraging words, then leaned down to untie the rope securing her to the gate. She offered no resistance whatsoever and was soon in the back of the van.

After a good towelling and a bowl of food, she had settled

down well. It took the merest bit of detective work to guess why she'd been abandoned.

She was about a year old and, to judge from her extended teats, had clearly recently given birth to puppies. This had obviously been inconvenient for her owner, who had abandoned her in the middle of nowhere. If it hadn't been for the farmer, she would almost certainly have died of hypothermia that night.

Consoling as it was to think we'd saved her from perishing, it was heartbreaking to consider what might have happened to her litter. Quite how we in Britain had come to call ourselves a nation of animal lovers was sometimes beyond my comprehension.

I knew it was highly unprofessional to laugh down the telephone at a caller, but when I heard why this rather grand-sounding lady had rung the RSPCA on a Friday evening I simply couldn't help myself.

'I'd like you to come and remove a stray peacock,' she said in plummy tones. 'He's bringing the family bad luck.'

Many animals and birds are the subject of superstition, but no creature is surrounded by so many amazingly silly beliefs as *Pavo cristata*, the peacock. Some folk will not have peacock feathers in the house, or even pictures of the birds on their walls. I once heard of an antiques dealer who wouldn't buy a pair of valuable vases purely because there were peacocks on the china.

I've never really understood what lay at the root of this superstition. Maybe it goes back to the ancient Greeks, whose artists portrayed the 'oceli' in the peacock's train as an 'evil eye'. Or perhaps it comes from more recent times when cottagers lived near large estates where peacocks were kept and allowed to roam at will, often no doubt even into the cottages' gardens, where they would have created havoc with early-season vegetables. It wouldn't surprise me if some cottager, after losing all his lettuces, spread the idea that peacocks were bad luck hoping to promote their downfall and the rumour had stuck.

They are certainly odd birds. Even though they have been bred in captivity for hundreds of years, they couldn't remotely be called domesticated. Quite the opposite, in fact. Peacocks retain just about all the characteristics of the wild Indian birds that first caught the fancy of the British upper classes centuries ago.

But, to my mind at least, all the superstitions surrounding them were utter nonsense. The lady on the other end of the telephone clearly thought differently.

'It's been here three weeks and ever since it arrived all sorts of strange things have happened,' she said. 'I've had far more breakages in the house than is usual, and today the car has a flat tyre. There have been all manner of other annoying little incidents and it's all down to that wretched bird.'

Tongue in cheek, I offered some sympathy. I wasn't going to bother one of the inspectors with something as silly as this, so I made an arrangement to collect the peacock myself the following Wednesday.

The following day, Saturday, however, the lady was back on the phone again.

'Do you suppose that you could come over right away to pick up this peacock? We are having so much trouble,' she said, obviously in even more of a flap than the day before. 'As if things weren't bad enough, my husband has just fallen off a ladder and broken his arm.'

This time I managed to suppress my laughter. I couldn't have fun at someone else's expense.

It was, however, simply impossible for me to get away over

the weekend, so I tried to persuade her to keep our original appointment for the Wednesday. Reluctantly she agreed.

I had two days of silence, but on the Tuesday there was a third call. This time the voice on the other end of the phone was a man, less aristocratic-sounding but, if anything, even more distressed. It turned out to be the lady's husband.

'Look,' he began, 'I'm not a superstitious kind of bloke, but we have had nothing but problems since that blasted peacock came here. First of all minor things going wrong, and then my arm, and now, to cap it all, the bloody house has caught fire.'

'Oh, my goodness,' I said, shocked.

The situation had now become very serious indeed and I realised I'd have to act. 'OK, I'll come straight away,' I told him.

It was far from the first peafowl I'd had to deal with. In recent years it had become rather the 'in thing' to keep one or two peafowl on properties with land or large gardens. There were problems, one of the most common being the noise they make during courtship. A calling male can be heard from over half a mile away. It also has a habit of making its strange, rather harsh call at night under the moon. So I had intervened in many a case where an owner was being threatened with legal action by sleep-deprived neighbours.

I knew that catching and transporting a peacock can present problems. Because of their long trains, they cannot be boxed up as other birds. The best way to carry them is in what we called a swan bag – a nylon sleeve with one end wider than the other. The bird is put headfirst into the sleeve from the wide end so that its head protrudes through the narrow end and its train hangs outside at the other. This ensures there is no danger of the delicate and easily damaged train being harmed.

Luckily, I had one such bag handy. I packed it and headed off. An hour or so later I reached the end of a secluded Cornish lane and turned into the grounds of a large country estate. The sunlight was streaming through the fresh young leaves of the beech trees and dancing on the nearby brook. The immaculate lawns were bordered by large stands of rhododendron and camellia. It was beautiful. A peacock certainly wouldn't look out of place here, I thought to myself.

The home, too, I could see, was magnificent – a large nineteenth-century manor house. Unfortunately, smoke was rising from part of it. There was still a fire engine there, its long, yellow rubber hoses threading their way in through the front door.

Thankfully, the fire was not as bad as it could have been, but two rooms had been burned out. Inside, old, charred beams were dripping with water from the firemen's hoses, and the walls were splattered with ash. The windows were broken, their frames blackened. It was a depressing sight.

Towards the back of the house, I discovered the owners, a middle-aged couple, who were – not surprisingly – in an extremely agitated state. They were covered in soot and grime, and were generally dishevelled after their efforts to rescue what items of furniture they could from the damaged part of the house.

We had a brief conversation in which I commiserated with them on their run of 'bad luck', in particular the blaze. Perhaps foolishly I tried to inject a little levity into things.

'Do you still blame the peacock for it all?' I asked.

The husband delivered his answer as plainly as he possibly could. 'Just get the bloody thing out of here,' he said, waving an arm as he headed back into the charred section of the house, doubtless in search of anything else that could be salvaged from the wreckage.

Outside, I soon spotted the peacock, sitting on the roof of the house, its blue neck brilliant in the noonday sun, its bright eyes gazing down at me. It looked magnificent, and I could see how these breathtaking good looks had persuaded the owners of the house to take the bird in. The love affair, however, was clearly over.

The problem was how to get hold of the unwanted peacock. He seemed quite content to stay on the roof, and there was no way that I could get hold of him while he remained on his lofty perch. I would have to wait until he decided to fly down into the garden.

To be honest, it wasn't the sort of garden anyone would have minded waiting in, full of interesting plants and a small lake where large golden orfe swam between clumps of crimson and yellow water lilies. It was idyllic.

At length, however, the peacock stood up, lazily stretched one wing, shook himself and then flew down from the roof into a paved courtyard surrounded by outbuildings. Now was my chance to nab him.

I knew from experience that you had to be canny to catch a peacock. A couple of years earlier I had been called out to catch two strays that had turned up at a plant nursery and were ravaging the vegetables and bedding plants. I managed to chivvy the pair into a long glasshouse and confidently went in to pick them up, when, to my horror, both birds took flight, flying at speed down the length of the glasshouse and straight through the panes of glass at the end.

The nursery owner was not amused.

This time I had come armed with a bag of corn. Having opened the door of a small toolshed behind the peacock, I put a handful of corn on the floor of the shed and laid a thin trail outside.

Fortunately, the bird was hungry and was soon pecking

away at the trail of corn until at last he was inside the shed. The moment the peacock was inside, I followed and quickly shut the door. I then got the bird safely into the swan bag. Mission accomplished.

I drove away wishing the couple better luck. They surely needed it.

CHAPTER SIXTEEN

Snip the Squatter Squirrel

One evening I was in the shelter at the rear of the house when I heard the sound of some kind of kerfuffle coming from the direction of the lane that passed the farm gate. I could make out the sound of a woman's voice, coupled with barks and growls. I could also pick out the telltale sound of a bird croaking.

Walking through the yard to see what the fuss was about, I heard a collection of faintly hysterical commands to 'sit', 'heel' and 'go away'. Reaching the lane, I saw a middle-aged woman looking rather like a maypole, completely wrapped around with dog leads, trying to control three Labradors who were threatening to trip her up at any moment.

It wasn't hard to work out who – or what – had driven her into this panicked state.

A copse of tall trees near the farm's entrance had become Odin the raven's favourite spot. He loved to dig around in the tree roots, hiding there all sorts of treasures that he'd collected: bits of coloured glass, bottle tops, in fact anything that took his fancy.

The trees that bordered the lane offered a good vantage point from which to watch the various comings and goings. It also allowed him to hide, undetected, before jumping out at unsuspecting walkers.

The ever-mischievous bird rarely missed an opportunity to capitalise on this and had done so again this evening, at this lady's expense. Just out of reach of the three Labradors' snapping jaws, Odin was dancing round and round, beak open, eyes gleaming, revelling in the mayhem he was causing. I ran to help the lady, cursing our devil bird to the heavens.

Odin's bad behaviour had been getting progressively worse. As well as pecking at people's bottoms, he'd completely mastered the art of throwing his voice. On more than one occasion he'd convinced Julie I was calling her from the farm. When she arrived at an empty spot, Odin would be there to chuckle away at her confusion. 'Where's Rex?' he'd say. 'Where's Rex?'

When his behaviour had become especially bad, I'd tried to keep him confined to the aviary. Even then, he managed to get up to no good. He would place pieces of bread just within reach of the chickens' beaks on the inside of the wire, tempting the poultry into his range. One or two bantams fell for the ruse and lost their heads as a result.

After a while even the poultry became wary and learned to

keep well away. It hadn't taken Odin long to work out a new strategy. He simply escaped from his prison cell.

Cement blocks had been laid around the base of the aviary to serve as a foundation, and one of these, smaller than the rest, had worked loose. Odin had spotted this and after much digging with his beak managed to prise the block away from the others, leaving a gap that he could just manage to squeeze through. He was soon back to his old tricks, as this evening had confirmed.

His behaviour towards this lady was beyond the pale, however, and demanded more serious measures. To prevent the delinquent bird from escaping again, I made sure his aviary was doubly secure and replaced the displaced concrete block with another one, this time firmly cemented in place.

'There, see how much mischief you can get up to now,' I muttered, as I left him croaking furiously at me.

Of course, the ideal solution would have been for him to fly away and join his own kind. But by now I was more convinced than ever that Odin was never going to leave us.

One morning a couple of weeks earlier I had been in the fields when his unmistakeable shape loomed into view in the sky. Odin was an exhibitionist at heart. At once he went into a tremendous display of flying, rolling and diving, then soaring up until he was just a black dot in the blue sky.

Unfortunately for Odin, he timed his aerobatic display badly. Suddenly there were three black dots in the sky. I guessed immediately the other two birds were the wild ravens from the cliffs a couple of miles away. Soon they were interacting, diving and chasing each other, making a tremendous din as they did so. Soon all three birds vanished from sight, still hundreds of feet up, over the inland hills.

I wondered whether this might be the big bird's downfall. We spent that evening vainly looking out for him.

The next day we got a call from a smallholder two miles away. He told us that the previous evening a large black bird had landed in the yard, chased the family dog and roosted on the barn roof. That morning the bird had been on the doorstep as the children left for school, squawking, 'Come on, then,' and nipping at their ankles. The father had managed to entice the raven into a stable, where he had promptly locked him in. It was pretty obvious it was Odin.

'If you'd like to collect him, that would be great,' the man said when I said the bird was mine. 'I don't want him upsetting my children again this evening.'

Odin was delighted when I collected him. In truth he had been very fortunate. He could so easily have been shot had he gone to an unfriendly farmer, instead of to the kindly folk who had taken the trouble to report him.

I felt sure that one day Odin's luck was going to run out.

The sight that greeted me as I walked into the yard one morning stopped me in my tracks.

Klair was standing by the entrance to one of the cages with a squirrel on her shoulder. Not only that, she was talking animatedly to the creature, repeatedly calling it by what I assumed was his name.

'Come on, Snip,' she said. 'Eat your breakfast, Snip.'

'Snip,' I muttered to myself. 'Since when was he called Snip? What on earth's going on here?'

The squirrel had come to us a few weeks earlier, the victim of a dog attack. He had been rescued from the canine's jaws and had been in a state of shock when he had arrived with us but had quickly recovered.

From the outset I'd noticed that the squirrel was unafraid of humans. The first time I opened the cage door, he had immediately jumped up on to my shoulder. This tameness suggested to me that he had been hand-reared.

Cute as he may have looked, this was not a good state of affairs. It remained one of our golden rules that wild animals should not be allowed to become domesticated. They would never survive in their natural environment if they became too used to human company. This was particularly important with squirrels, which make very poor pets.

Squirrels have extremely strong chisel-like teeth, which they can't stop trying out on just about everything they come into contact with, including humans. When they are very young, nibbling away at people's fingers, it is not so much of a threat. But as a squirrel matures it can become short-tempered and can inflict really bad wounds. Park-dwelling wild grey squirrels that have become overconfident with humans have been known to attack and bite the people feeding them.

To be fair, this squirrel had shown no signs of aggression, hence the favouritism being bestowed upon him by the girls. But seeing that he had now been given a name proved things had gone too far.

Seeing Klair playing with Snip, or whatever his name was, confirmed something else too. The demands of running the communications centre meant that I had much less time to concentrate on my responsibilities to the animals. I'd worried for a while that this was having an adverse effect on things at the sanctuary. This proved to me that it was. I would need to address it.

Right now, however, my priority was this squirrel. It was perhaps no wonder that he'd been damaged by a dog. He hadn't learned the survival skills he would have picked up living on his wits in the local woods. If he was going to have any chance of a long life, he would have to go back into the wild. And now was as good a time as any for that to happen, I decided.

Grey squirrels, originally from America, have driven out and decimated the native red squirrels in this country. Today it is illegal to release grey squirrels into the wild, but for many years it was not. Later that day, with Julie covering the phone for me, I released the squirrel into the woods at the end of the farmland about half a mile away from the house.

Snip seemed happy to be there and scurried around, climbing trees and obviously enjoying himself. He was exploring the uppermost branches of a tall ash tree when I quietly turned on my heel and hurried away back to the farm.

I headed back, relieved that this potential problem had been nipped in the bud. As if things were ever that easy. As I let myself through the gate from the fields, I heard a flurry of activity high in the hazel trees. There, to my surprise, I saw Snip jumping through the branches.

Before I knew it he'd dropped to the lowest branch and taken a flying leap on to my shoulder, where he settled down chittering to himself as if to say, 'That was really something. Now let's go home.'

Great, I thought. Another squatter who doesn't want to move out.

We stepped out into the early-morning light nervously, unsure of what we were going to encounter.

Throughout the day before, the wind had been building. As nightfall had set in, Radio Cornwall had issued storm warnings with forecasts of force-ten gales and winds in excess of 100 miles per hour. As we'd lain in bed, it sounded as if an army of giants was wreaking havoc outside. All night there were strange crashes and thumps, the sound of splintering timber and roof tiles crashing into the yard.

We were braced for the worst, but the scene that greeted us in the daylight was still unbelievable. The chicken houses and their residents had been lifted by the wind and thrown yards across the fields before being smashed to pieces. The bodies of birds were scattered everywhere, many of them impaled by the flying timbers. Turning back to inspect the house from the fields, I saw that part of the roof had vanished, its tiles broken and lying in heaps on the ground below.

Wherever we turned the picture was one of carnage. Most of the large evergreen conifers in the area had been blown down, including those that had stood in these exposed coastal gardens for up to a century. Moving through the fields, we found our cattle terrified. Some were huddled in the lea of hedges, while others had sought shelter in barns. The whole world seemed torn apart – unfriendly and unfamiliar.

It was then that I noticed the large, heavy aviary where Odin had been caged. The flight had been lifted from its block base in one corner and was now resting on its side. Odin had gone, panicked no doubt by the fury of the gale.

To judge by the damage to the outbuildings, the birds would not have been able to deal with the force of the wind. I imagined that many would have been killed by the gale's fury, including our rascal of a raven.

I called Ralph Gardner immediately, requesting a day or two off telephone duties so that I could start work rebuilding the sanctuary. He kindly agreed to take over the phone for me.

It was a couple of days later that, quite by chance, a local pig farmer called to see us. We'd made a start on putting the sheds and cages back together again and I was at work on the big aviary. When I mentioned it had housed our raven, the farmer told me about a crow that had been following his tractor the previous day.

'Huge thing with a hell of a beak on it,' he said. 'It sat on the canopy chatting away. Couldn't stop talking. It was amazing, really.'

There was only one bird that could elicit that sort of reaction. Immediately Julie, the girls and I jumped into the van and drove over to the field where the farmer had last seen the 'crow'.

We arrived as dusk was falling. There was no sign of Odin, but there were plenty of trees in which he might be roosting. I walked over to them and shone a torch up into the branches. Sure enough, Odin was there, perched near the crown of the tallest tree, looking apprehensive, his plumage held tightly to his body, ready to fly off at the first hint of danger.

He was a shadow of his former self. Obviously he had been badly frightened by his experience and was not in a trusting mood.

The pig farmer, Julie and the girls had by now gathered behind me.

'How are you going to get him down?' Zoë asked.

I thought about it for a moment, then realised there was only one thing to do. At the risk of appearing a complete idiot, I took a few paces back from the tree and called out in a loud, but hopefully endearing voice, 'Odin, come to Daddy.'

The bird's response was immediate. With a loud, happy croak he dropped from the tree like a bundle of black rags, landing at my feet. Normally he hated to be picked up, but on this occasion he was more than happy to be scooped into my arms.

He was soon safely installed back in his aviary. There had been plenty of occasions when I'd wished he was no longer part of the furniture at Ferndale. This time, however, I couldn't have been happier to have him home. His presence signalled a return to normality.

Snip the squirrel was proving as determined to stay with us as our indestructible raven.

Since my first failed attempt to send him back into the woods, I'd tried to let him loose several times. On one occasion I'd enlisted Julie's help. Together, we'd gone to the trouble of climbing an ash tree with him. We'd both sat there for almost half an hour, hoping eventually he'd come to regard the tree as a suitable new home. After a while he'd settled down nicely and had become engaged in a game of chase with a younger grey squirrel. Sensing our chance, we'd climbed down, headed back to the house and forgotten all about him.

Our respite had lasted for around three hours. Checking the shelter that night, I'd discovered his familiar features on the roof.

Julie had recently made our last attempt to get rid of him. She'd been heading off to Perranporth to see some friends and had intended walking through the woods at the end of our land en route. She had taken Snip with her and had left him climbing happily around in the trees, convinced he had finally seen the benefits of a life in the wild.

It had been the following morning that he'd returned, this time in the most unlikely fashion. Somehow Snip had managed to persuade a cyclist to let him sit on his shoulder. Goodness knows whether the squirrel had known what would happen, but predictably the chap had headed for Ferndale.

I'd been out on the lane and was struck dumb by the sight of the pair of them rolling down the hill towards us.

I don't believe it, I had thought to myself. I've seen everything now.

Today, however, I was certain Snip was finally leaving us for good. I put him in the back of the van and began the nine-mile drive to Tehidy Park, a large wooded area on the coast near Redruth.

Open to the public, who came to enjoy the scenery and also to have close encounters with its wildlife, Tehidy Park has several lakes with waterfowl and wild birds of all kinds. There is also a large colony of grey squirrels.

I'd figured that if Snip was ever going to reacquaint himself with the rest of the squirrel population, it would be by joining in a large community. It would be easier for him to blend in there. He would also get a fair deal of human attention. Tehidy Park is popular with families, who would bring peanuts and other snacks for the squirrels to feed on.

Sure enough, no sooner had I set Snip down on the ground than he was joining a small group of other squirrels cadging peanuts from an elderly lady sitting on a bench. I watched for a while, to make sure there was no adverse reaction from the other squirrels. But they seemed oblivious to the fact Snip was a newcomer to the park. He blended in with the rest of the community seamlessly and was soon chasing a couple of younger squirrels round the trunk of a large oak tree.

Rehabilitating wild animals could be a fairly straightforward process, but as I'd discovered with Snip, it could be the devil's own work as well.

As I headed back to the van I felt quietly confident that this time, finally, I'd reintroduced him to his natural habitat and that he would stay there for good. He did. I never saw our squatter squirrel again.

CHAPTER SEVENTEEN
Swanning Around

The RSPCA inspector parked his van in the yard, climbed out and swung open the back doors. I took one look inside and started shaking my head slowly and rather ruefully.

'Oh, dear,' I said under my breath.

Inside was an adult mute swan that appeared more dead than alive, head down and eyes closed. The inspector told me it had been found not far away, on the coast just outside Perranporth, where it had flown into overhead power lines.

The massive voltage had left it stunned and extensively bruised, but so far as I could tell from a quick examination, it had suffered no broken bones.

As Britain's largest and heaviest flying bird, swans are prime candidates for accidents, particularly when they are flying around, as they do in the autumn, when young swans are chased away from their homes by their parents in advance of next spring's breeding season.

At this time of the year it was quite common for them to collide with tall buildings, power cables and pylons. In addition, swans flying in fog or following heavy rain often mistake glistening roads for rivers and crash-land on to them. They then get stranded, unable to take off from the hard surface.

My main concern today was that this was the first swan casualty to arrive at Ferndale. I'd dealt with plenty of displaced cygnets over the years, but this was a different matter entirely. This bird needed intensive-care treatment, and I wasn't sure I was equipped to provide it. For a start, I didn't have a cage large enough to accommodate a swan that needed heat treatment from an infrared lamp.

But I couldn't say no. I would have to do the best I could.

At least swans weren't unknown to me. In fact, away from the farm, I'd had my fair share of encounters with them, all of them memorable in their own way.

One that always sticks in my mind happened down in the south-coast town of Fowey. I'd been called out to aid a pair of swans that had built a nest in a reed-bed at the edge of a lake in the grounds of a large estate. Unfortunately for them, the area was also populated by foxes. The estate's gamekeeper had acted on this and erected a stock fence, lined with barbed wire on top, to protect the birds.

The fox is a resourceful and cunning creature, as we all know. Somehow, on the day the eggs were due to hatch, a fox managed to get through the fence, doubtless having heard the hatching cygnets chirping in the eggs. His arrival scared the mother, or pen, so badly that she panicked and joined her mate, or cob, out on the lake.

The results were predictable – and grisly. I was called in by the owner of the estate and arrived to discover that the fox had eaten two of the eggs and that the other four had rolled out of the nest into the reeds.

I could tell from the weak cheeping coming from the eggs that at least one or two of the unhatched cygnets were still alive and so decided to try to return the eggs to the nest in the hope their mother would come back to complete their incubation.

The challenge was to straddle the barbed-wire fence, gather up the eggs and replace them. I knew I would have to do this without antagonising the swans. In most cases, swans have extremely gentle natures. They are distinctly less easy-going during the breeding season, however, when pairs of swans make formidably protective parents.

The cob, in particular, can be a fearsome creature, and it's not advisable to cross him in any way. Dogs, foxes and other waterfowl that dare to threaten a swan's nest can be attacked and in some cases even drowned by the defensive birds. Humans, too, can be attacked, sometimes unintentionally.

I was once involved in a case where a man rescued a swan's nest that was in danger of being swept away on a high tide from reed-beds at the bottom of his riverside garden. Taking a boat out, he crossed the river and managed to secure the nest with ropes tied on to nearby willows. The adult swans meanwhile had been watching the action from further up the river. They were a young, inexperienced pair, which accounted for their poor choice of nest site and their lack of effort in protecting it; however, as the rescuer of their nest and eggs was rowing his way back across the river, the young cob decided that he had better take a stand and flew downstream close to the boat and in passing caught the bow with his wing,

197

tipping the boat over and its occupant into the river. Consequently, I kept a close eye on the cob as I tried to retrieve the four eggs.

I managed it – just. It proved a painful process as I had to straddle the fence with the sharp barbed wire digging into me in the most vulnerable spot imaginable.

Just as I was about to disentangle myself, both swans attacked me. They flew in at speed, lashing with their wings and causing a miniature tidal wave along the way.

What ensued can't have looked very edifying. Still straddling the fence and balancing precariously on one foot, I grabbed both flailing swans by their necks, one in each hand, and waited for them to settle down. When they had calmed a little, I managed with some difficulty to pick them up and tuck one under each arm. Somehow extricating myself from the barbed wire, I took the two birds back on to the lake and released them.

The good news was that the four remaining eggs did hatch safely and the cygnets grew up to be fine, healthy swans. My injuries turned out to be minimal and in no way inhibited my private life, although it was a close thing! I'd had a lucky escape.

Swans are, of course, the subject of much mythology. Perhaps the most widely held belief is that males and females pair for life and will pine and die if a partner is killed. On the evidence of another encounter I had, this isn't really the case.

Another elderly pair of swans resident on the Fowey river were well known to me. The rather large cob was known for his complete intolerance of any other waterfowl that invaded his territory. One day the old chap was busily involved with chasing off some trespassing swans, which took to the air closely followed by the irate cob. So intent was he on seeing off the intruders that he failed to look where he was flying and flew too close to a moored yacht, colliding with the mast and crashing down on to the deck. The heavy fall nearly finished him off. However, he survived and, after several weeks' care at an RSPCA centre, was returned to the river and his mate.

Unfortunately, during his absence the pen had found herself a toy boy. And far from being pleased to see her old partner, she attacked him with some vigour, aided and abetted by her new love.

The poor old cob had to be rescued once again or he would certainly have been murdered.

Swans had provided me with some fun moments, none more memorable than the one when I helped an RSPCA colleague in a rescue at a local nature reserve.

The lake there had become completely overgrown with an exotic plant called *Myriophyllum aquaticum*, commonly known as parrot feather. The water had been drained from the lake through a lock gate, leaving just a small pond in the centre of the area, in the middle of which was an island made from wooden pallets. A pair of swans had nested and hatched five cygnets on this precarious spot.

The idea had been to drain the lake in full and then to get a digger to clear out all the silt and weed, allowing the lake to be replenished with fresh water. Things hadn't gone according to plan, however, and the JCB had become stuck in the deep mud, almost up to the sides of the cab. In the end it had to be hauled out by a tractor.

As a result of this the swans and their very young cygnets had been left stranded. The young birds had no chance of climbing the steep mudbanks at the lake's edge, and their parents weren't capable of helping them out.

I arrived with an inspector, Mike, and quickly saw that we were faced with crossing the sixty feet of deep, oozing mud that separated the shore from the swans' island. No one seemed to know how deep the mud was, but given the fact the JCB had been almost completely submerged, I didn't think a human stood much chance of crossing it.

After much debate it was decided to try laying long planks out across the mud to make a walkway. When this was finished, Mike and I edged our way out over the squelching, oozing, black mud.

Unfortunately, there were not enough planks to reach all the way to the island. We were about fifteen feet short. On reaching the end of the walkway, we decided to pick up the plank that we had just walked on and place it ahead of us so that we could continue on our precarious way.

When, at long last, we reached the island, we discovered the pen alone guarding her cygnets. Naturally she eyed us with suspicion.

I edged slowly towards her and her family and once within range swiftly grabbed four cygnets. After quickly passing them back to my colleague, I just managed to catch the fifth as it was about to jump into the water.

The pen was rather taken by surprise by all this sudden action and was slow to defend her cygnets. When she did react it was too late. Mike quickly caught her and popped her into a swan bag.

The cob had been swimming on the pond until now. Seeing what was going on, he came ashore at speed, ready to attack. He was also too late, and soon found himself caught with a swan hook and packed into another carrying bag.

Mike and I felt quite pleased with ourselves and were all smiles as we made our return journey across the mud, balancing precariously on the planks with swans and cygnets tucked under our arms or carried in boxes.

Despite these sometimes hair-raising adventures, I was fond of swans. I knew that on their own and out of the breeding season, they were gentle-natured animals. And so it proved with our first swan casualty as she recovered from her rather shocking experience with the overhead power line. In the days and weeks that followed her arrival with us, the injured swan proved easy to handle and offered no resistance to the treatment I gave her.

I hadn't been sure where to put her at first. I didn't want her to intimidate or agitate any of the other birds. So for her first few days I put her in an empty chicken house, where she could recover from the trauma of her electrocution.

Slowly the extensive bruising on her body started to fade. After a week or so she perked up considerably. I decided to let her out with the domestic ducks and geese, which worked well. There was plenty of grass to go around, and the large water containers were full so there were no confrontations of any kind. The swan simply got on with its own business, grazing with the geese until the evening, when I would shepherd her back into the chicken house for the night.

I learned much about swans from this particular bird, not least the rather surprising fact that they love being talked to.

I noticed how when I spoke to her in the morning, the swan would respond, bowing her head and walking alongside me. I built on this, encouraging her, rather like a dog, to walk to heel as I fed the other waterfowl. Swans are semi-domesticated and can be treated as such – unlike all truly wild birds there is no need to keep them at arm's length. Invariably swans are released in areas where they will be in close contact with the public and reliant on people for at least part of their food.

By the time she'd been with us a month or so, I'd become quite attached to her, although I knew she would soon have to be released back into the wild. That day arrived rather sooner than I thought.

I was walking across the fields back towards the house late

one afternoon when I heard a sound I recognised almost immediately. The rhythmic singing of a swan's wings in full flight is one of the most distinctive and beautiful in all of nature as far as I'm concerned. I turned round just in time to see the elegant white bird flying low in a large circle over the top end of the farm.

Good girl. Another satisfied customer ready to leave us, I thought, feeling rather pleased with myself.

I watched the swan circling, her wings flapping with seemingly little effort like a metronome, and knew her time with us was over. I decided to take her back to the river the following day. As it turned out, I wouldn't get the chance.

That evening, at dusk, as the geese were coming in for the night, the swan took wing once more. This time it flew off up the valley and disappeared behind some trees at the end of a neighbour's field. The swan had only just skimmed the tops of the trees and I was not sure that it had managed to remain airborne, so I rushed off in the same direction to see if she had landed and needed help. But there was no sign of her.

I must admit I spent part of the night worrying about her. The following day I waited slightly nervously for reports of a wandering swan, but none came. I assumed that she had managed to gain height and eventually got back to the river Fal, eight miles away.

For some reason, however, I couldn't quite rest easy. I felt I should go out into the fields where she'd headed the previous evening to make sure she wasn't hurt. To my relief, I saw no sign of her. At last I was satisfied that she must indeed have made her escape and headed homewards.

By the time I'd turned for home, it was nearly dark. I'd crossed several fields and decided that the shortest way back was along an overgrown lane. All went well until, at the very end of the lane, I was confronted with a makeshift gate. It was made up of two ancient bedsprings, one on top of the other, which my neighbour had constructed to keep his cattle from straying into the lane.

Climbing over the obstacle with some difficulty, I jumped down into the field on the far side, but not quickly enough to escape the top bedspring, which had come loose and crashed down on top of me, knocking me flat.

As I struggled out from under the bedspring I was aware of a lot of blood streaming down my face. I realised a piece of the metal had hit me on the nose, causing a rather painful wound.

When I got home and looked in the mirror, I saw that my nose was completely skinned. The flesh was hanging down in a large flap. Julie took one look and phoned our GP, who told me to come over to the surgery, which he was going to open up especially for me.

'The things some people will do to look after birds,' he muttered, anaesthetising my nose, placing the torn skin back in place, then using a large needle and some thick black thread to insert a line of sutures.

I must admit I got some very strange looks over the coming days and weeks. With thick black stitches sticking out from my nose, I must have looked like some kind of desperado.

Eventually the wound healed well, but it was obvious I was going to remain scarred for life. To this day the mark is there, a reminder of the pleasures and pitfalls of dealing with swans.

CHAPTER EIGHTEEN
Biology Lessons

Outside, the wind was howling and the rain bucketing down, so the sound of someone knocking at the front door late one evening gave me a start.

'That sounds like trouble,' I said to Julie, assuming it must be a real emergency for someone to call on such a filthy night.

To my relief, I found the dripping-wet figure of Ralph Gardner standing on the doorstep, his imposing figure silhouetted against the thin moonlight.

'Evening, Rex. Sorry to bother you so late,' the chief inspector said, removing his sodden cap. 'Do you mind if I come in for a moment? I've got a bit of news.'

'Of course, Ralph,' I said, ushering him into the kitchen,

where Julie was clearing up the dinner things.

'Oh, hello, Ralph,' she said. 'Cup of tea?'

'Please, Julie. I could do with some warming up.'

In the years since we'd got to know him, Ralph had become a close personal friend as well as a professional colleague. Above all he'd been the most valuable adviser we'd had, a ready source of wisdom when problems arose.

Ralph had never been a man for small talk so he wasted no time in relating his news.

'I don't know if you remember those plans we had to build a centre for the whole of Cornwall. I think we were talking about it when you first moved here,' he said.

'Er, yes, but remind me,' I mumbled.

'You know, the oiled-bird cleaning centre, the big cattery and the office block . . .'

'Oh, yes, of course,' I said, recalling vaguely what had been said when Julie and I had first met the RSPCA committee. To be honest, I'd put it to the back of my mind. It had seemed something of a pipe dream to me.

'Well, it looks like it's finally going to happen,' Ralph said, fixing me with a wide smile. 'We've come into rather a lot of money. A lady over in Truro passed away and left us her estate. Quite a tidy sum.'

'Oh, that's great, Ralph,' I said, still unsure what this had to do with us.

'I've just come from a special meeting of the committee, and we've decided we'd like to use the money to build the centre,' he said.

Clearly there was something in my face that told him the penny hadn't quite dropped. Julie, too, was silent, still lost in her chores at the other end of the room.

'We'd like to build the centre here at Ferndale, Rex.'

'Here?' Julie said, turning round.

As both Julie and I stood there looking dumbfounded and unable to respond, Ralph fished into his briefcase and produced a large folded piece of paper. He then laid out on the kitchen table what looked like the plans for a small housing development. It turned out to be the blueprint for Cornwall's first animal centre.

Julie and I sat at the table as Ralph explained that the RSPCA were willing to buy a section of the land at Ferndale.

'This bit below the old barn, where it runs along the road,' he said, indicating an area marked in blue on the map where the buildings were concentrated. The half-acre site was to be developed to include an L-shaped office, a large cattery and a specialist oiled-bird cleaning unit. The rest of the site would be lined with aviaries and other cages.

'Naturally you'd still have the field shelter for other animals as well, Rex,' Ralph explained. 'And the communications centre would move from here into the office, where there would be a full-time receptionist.'

It was certainly an impressive-looking plan, but, truth be told, it was a little too much to take in, especially when it had come out of the blue like this.

Ralph knew us well enough to see this.

'Obviously it's up to you and Julie, Rex,' he said. 'Why don't you two take a few days to talk it over? Get back to me as quickly as you can.'

He was soon folding up his plans and heading off into the rain.

Julie and I sat up late that night, talking over the pros and cons of what Ralph had proposed. We both agreed that in many ways it was what we'd always dreamed of – a proper, fully funded animal sanctuary – and more besides. But the fact the RSPCA were going to acquire some of our land hadn't really been part of our plans. Nor had we really thought about our sanctuary being staffed by outsiders.

'How many people will be working here?' Julie wondered. 'And who will they be?'

We agreed to sleep on it. But I think we both went to bed with our minds made up.

I called Ralph back the following morning.

'Well, we'd like to say yes,' I told him. 'I do have one or two questions, though.'

The plan for the development of the centre presented me with something of a dilemma. I'd been running the Cornish RSPCA's communications centre for a couple of years, but in the months before Ralph had come to see me I'd been led to believe the funding for it might not last much longer. So when I'd heard of a job back at the Post Office, driving a van, I'd taken it, juggling the two jobs for a while but eventually giving in my notice to the RSPCA. Plans for a full-scale centre obviously changed things once more. I was anxious to know where I stood.

Talking to Ralph the following day, it became clear the warden of the new centre wouldn't be eligible for a full salary, at least to begin with.

'It would be a nominal salary,' he said. 'We'd be looking for a volunteer really, Rex,' he said. 'At least while we build up the operation, which is going to take a year or two.'

I simply couldn't afford to do that and told Ralph as much.

He mulled it over for a few moments, then came up with another suggestion. 'How about if we made you a voluntary warden as well, Rex, but with responsibility for the place when the office was closed?' he said. 'That way, you could carry on at the Post Office in the daytime, then take over in the evenings. We'd pay you what we could of course.'

This sounded good to me and we agreed. I also agreed to

help him in looking for a volunteer warden to get the centre off the ground.

'Great,' Ralph said. 'I'll get things rolling.'

In the weeks that followed, things moved fast.

It turned out that the RSPCA's bequest had come from a lady called Agnes Clark. She'd been a lifelong supporter with a particular interest in cats. As the plans firmed up over the ensuing weeks, one of the first decisions taken was that the new oiled-bird centre, the first building to be erected, should be named after her.

Memories of the awful *Torrey Canyon* oil spill, back in 1967, remained clear in Cornwall, and there had been many other smaller-scale incidents since that tanker had run aground disgorging millions of gallons of oil on to the Cornish coast. When the newspapers reported the bequest that had made a bird-cleaning centre possible, the local RSPCA suddenly found themselves being donated even more money. It meant that things moved on even more quickly than originally planned.

The area of land alongside the road was soon alive with workmen. Within weeks Cornwall's first official animal centre was taking shape. Finding the right staff for the new centre wasn't going to be easy, I knew that.

Many people are attracted to the idea of working with animals in theory. In practice, however, few think through the realities. The potential glamour of the job wears a little thin when you are cleaning out kennels, avoiding being bitten by aggressive dogs or having cats vomit down the front of your clean overalls. But the reality is this is all part of the job.

So when Ralph and his colleagues advertised for staff for the new centre, there was no shortage of people – mainly, it has to be said, girls – who turned up clearly intent on rescuing every animal on earth.

Ralph knew it wasn't hard to root out the ones who were unsuited. The news that as well as grooming lovely cats and dogs they would also have to deal with sick and possibly aggressive animals laid the first seeds of doubt. The realisation that some cats and dogs would not be suitable for adoption and would face euthanasia would put them off completely.

Interviewees travelled from all over the county in the hope of getting the job. In the end, however, we found the person we needed right under our noses. Annie lived locally with her parents and was down to earth, hard-working and a fastidious organiser. She would work each day from eight until six, at which point I would take over from her.

Her job in many ways was the one I'd been doing over the years. She would oversee the welfare of the inmates in our various pens and cages, liaise with the RSPCA inspectors out on the road and provide the first point of contact with the public.

Annie was kept on her toes all day long. News of a new expanded centre drew in even more calls and visitors. It wasn't long before the branch decided to take on another assistant – Annie's mum, known to one and all as Mrs K.

As the new-look centre found its feet, we began to attract a regular stream of work-experience students as well, many of them pupils from local schools. These often proved a distinct mixed blessing. Some children clearly thought working at the centre would be a soft option. They imagined stroking kittens and puppies all day. But while some became disillusioned when they found themselves scrubbing floors, others took a genuine interest and proved excellent helpers.

Inevitably we had some volunteers who thought they knew it all.

One young chap from near Perranporth turned up claiming he had extensive experience looking after dogs. Rather foolishly, I took him at his word and sent him out on his first morning to exercise three rescue dogs. I told him to take a route that was about two miles long around the local lanes.

It was only half an hour or so later that I was driving past a nearby holiday village. Out of the corner of my eye, I saw three dogs rushing around between the chalets. I recognised them immediately: they were the rescue trio from the centre. I pulled up and headed towards them.

'What the hell are you up to?' I asked the so-called helper. 'You told me you understood dogs.'

'I do,' he said defensively.

'How can you?' I said. 'If you did, you wouldn't let three rescue dogs run wild like that. They could have got into all sorts of trouble.'

'I thought they needed a run,' he said defiantly. 'Besides, you should have trained them to come when someone calls them.'

Needless to say, his services were not called upon again.

Since taking in the very first animals at the Rosery, I'd known that experience was the greatest teacher. So it proved again as Ferndale entered a new and much more demanding era.

Unsurprisingly, the opening of the new oiled-bird cleaning unit provided us with the most vivid lessons. The facility was a purpose-built wooden hut, with deep stainless-steel sinks, tiled floors and walls lined with metal so as to remain as hygienic as possible. We were also armed with an array of high-powered sprays and nozzles, along with a variety of cleaning fluids.

When the first batch of oiled birds came in to us that winter, 1982–83, we relied on all the help we could get. My sons, Glen and Alan, spent what spare time they had during the holidays helping out, driving a specially adapted three-wheeler van around the beaches picking up some of the hundreds of oiled birds that had landed on the north Cornish beaches. We also relied on the small army of voluntary workers who were ready to help out in times of crisis.

Two local ladies, Maggie and Lesley, came along on two mornings a week to help. It was a task that required training, and dedication too. Thanks to the unofficial team leader, another local lady, Nan, there were always a team of trainees ready to come in and be shown the ropes.

There was much to learn. Ornithologists and conservationists had discovered a lot about treating oil-soaked birds in the wake of the *Torrey Canyon* disaster. The well-meaning people who had spent endless hours cleaning the birds caught up in that spill had made some serious, if unintentional mistakes. Not the least of their errors was the fact they'd released birds back on to the sea almost immediately after cleaning. When healthy, a bird's plumage is waterproof. But having been cleaned, the plumage needs to dry out and return to full health before regaining its waterproof qualities.

The *Torrey Canyon* birds were released before this process had happened properly. Many birds got waterlogged and, as a result, were unable to fly or swim back to shore and drowned.

In the years that followed the disaster, however, a viable new treatment had been developed by a team from Newcastle University. A simple washing-up liquid was now used to wash the oil from the plumage. The birds were then sprayed with warm water to remove the soap and any remaining oil. Birds usually required two such washes, after which they spent some time on the testing ponds to ensure that they were waterproof. It meant the birds were kept in care a little longer, but they eventually returned to the wild with, hopefully, a far better chance of survival.

As we got the new unit up and running, our first arrivals

included a great northern diver, a fairly uncommon winter visitor. It was not easy to treat. A diver's legs are set so far back on its body that it is a tremendous effort for the bird to walk on land. Normally the best it can do is to shuffle along on its breast feathers. This presents a real problem when you wash it. Once it has been given its final wash and waterproofing with the pressure spray, the bird's weight on the breast feathers tends to press the plumage flat and inhibit the drying process.

To overcome this problem, we placed the diver on a metal grid over a sink, then finished the waterproofing by spraying the warm water up through the grid until all the feathers had beaded and were dry. The bird was then placed in a small pen on a bed of towels to rest for several hours. It seemed to go well, and after being tested for waterproofing in the pond, we released it at Hayle, where there was a large land-locked pool fed by the sea at high tide and filled with large numbers of eels and crabs. Divers would generally spend a few days there before returning to sea.

During this first winter we also received large numbers of storm petrels. No bigger than a sparrow, these frail-looking birds seem unlikely candidates to withstand the fury of the Atlantic Ocean. And yet they are masters of flight, flitting like swallows just above the surface of the sea, often with their feet touching the water, feeding on plankton and tiny fish. Only the severest of storms brings them inland.

I knew this already, but we had to tell our new staff to be careful not to injure the petrels' delicate wings. Feeding them was a problem, too. In the end we found the best way to do this was by tube-feeding them on a diet of scraped fish and frozen plankton.

Petrels are mainly nocturnal birds so we found it best to release them in the late evening. This also helped avoid attacks by gulls. There was something rather magical about releasing them. They would fly away into the dusk, their dark colouration and erratic flight making them appear like bats in the torch beam.

Our victims didn't come exclusively from the sea.

Birds arrived at the cleaning unit covered in all sorts of substances. At various times we had a budgerigar covered in butter and a zebra finch that flew into a frying pan of warm fat. There were also victims of diesel spills on the roads. The diesel would sometimes seep into local ponds and streams, where the fuel would contaminate ducks, moorhens and coots, often in considerable numbers. This in particular left us facing a steep learning curve.

Diesel oil is very difficult to wash out of feathers, and birds can be badly affected by inhaling the fumes. Often, we discovered, the best solution was to house the birds in large pens in a well-ventilated room or, if the weather was fine enough, outdoors and simply let the oil 'weather' off the plumage naturally.

Swans were particularly vulnerable to the various substances that seeped into the rivers and lakes. We took in swans soaked in liquids ranging from sump oil and diesel to household cooking oil.

We learned that while they are big birds to wash, swans make good patients and are usually surprisingly gentle. They were also relatively easy to clean and rehabilitate. When dealing with a single oiled swan, we would often complete the drying process with a hairdryer. If there were several birds, we would place them in large indoor pens with a fan heater blowing warm air overhead and let them preen and put their feathers in order themselves.

As semi-domestic birds, the swans took well to captivity so there was never as great a rush to release them as there was with other, wilder birds. We would often keep them in our outside compound for a week before returning them to the wild.

Rehabilitating the swans to their natural environment was usually the trickiest part of the process. Being highly territorial, swans should always be returned to the place where they were picked up, if this is possible. If this isn't, or their place of origin was unknown, the next best option was to release them in neutral areas where there were no breeding pairs of swans.

We learned, however, that swans have a very definite idea of where they want to be. So even if you chose the most lavishly appointed lakes or ponds, they would fly off a few hours later if it wasn't to their liking. Clipping their wings wasn't an option. Unless they were somehow fenced in, the swans would simply walk away, leaving them vulnerable to foxes and dogs.

So over time we discovered that if a return to the original home wasn't possible, the best option was an estuary where herds of non-breeding swans congregated. They seemed to integrate well there, quickly fitting in without any hassle.

Of course, we learned the biggest lessons through the mistakes we made. And there were plenty of them.

One valuable lesson early on was delivered by some gannets. They are very nervous birds when first taken into captivity. When we tried to feed them in small indoor pens they became exceedingly anxious.

The distance human keepers need to put between themselves and captive wild animals before those animals relax is known as the flight distance. This is especially important when one is dealing with extremely nervous animals such as antelope and deer, and some birds of prey. For example, perching birds feel much safer if they are kept in cages positioned above human head height. This helps reduce panic, as birds hate people staring at them directly or towering over their cages. They can become agitated and do themselves harm in the process.

We learned that for the gannets to settle down and feed on their meals of mackerel, we had to enlarge their pens so that they were at least eight feet from us. This flight distance shortened as they relaxed in captivity, and after a while they would come to the front of their enclosure to accept fish.

By far the biggest mistake I made during the early days of the oiled-bird cleaning centre came when we got our first puffin. Puffins are a lot smaller than most people imagine, and this little chap arrived encased in a sheath of oil. We were able to clean and waterproof him easily enough and put him out on one of the small test ponds, where he swam around happily, bathing and preening himself.

Unfortunately, I'd forgotten that there was no overhead netting on this particular pond. No sooner had I turned my back than a greater-backed gull spotted the little black-and-white bird. To my horror, I turned to see him swoop down and swallow the puffin whole. I never put a small bird in that pool again.

In a similar vein, during our early days at the centre, one of the new assistants, Sue, and I reared a nest of greenfinches. Once they were fledged, we decided to transfer them to an aviary prior to release.

It was a lovely bright morning when we made the decision. We realised, however, that the aviaries were pretty full so had to make room for the new arrivals first. While we organised things we put the greenfinches in a large wire cage on the lawn, partially covering it with a cloth to protect the birds from the sun.

They seemed quite content there, so when lunchtime

arrived we left them for an hour or so. When Sue and I returned after lunch, all that remained of the young birds were a few feathers. A magpie had descended and frightened the finches so much they had fluttered up against the side of the cage, allowing the tenacious predator to easily pull them through the gaps in the wires. Sue was distraught at the discovery, and I could have kicked myself – very hard. Again, it was a mistake never to be repeated.

The sun was dipping behind the hills towards the coast, turning the evening sky into radiant shades of red. It was going to be a fine day tomorrow, that was for sure. Ordinarily, dusk was the signal for me to wind down things on the farm, to make my final checks and turn in for the night. Not tonight, however.

It was rare we got visitors after the centre closed unless they were emergencies. This evening we were expecting two very different callers. Our first guests were a group of Brownies from somewhere near Newquay, to whom I was going to give a talk about the work we did at Ferndale and the RSPCA in general.

I was a strong believer in talking to people, especially youngsters, in this way. By sparking an interest in animal welfare or perhaps answering a specific question, I might provide the knowledge that made life easier for some animals.

This evening the Brownies' visit coincided with that of a pig farmer from nearby Wadebridge who was coming over with his prize boar. The boar's task was to breed with our resident sow, Sally.

In the years since we'd moved to Ferndale, the farming side of our life had grown quite nicely. After successfully introducing goats and cows, we'd branched out into sheep and then a pig.

Our first pig, Sally, wasn't any old porker, she was a prime pedigree example of the breed Gloucester Old Spot. A long-established breed that had undergone something of a revival in popularity, Old Spots used to be known as orchard pigs. This harked back to the days when they lived on estates and were given the job of clearing up the fallen fruit under the orchard trees. They were claimed by those who knew the breed to be hardy, trouble-free animals, so when we heard of a local farmer who was breeding them, we jumped at the chance to get one.

The piglet we were offered was eight weeks old. She was small and pink with one or two black spots on her head and back and the happy expression that all piglets have. We christened her Sally, made her a shelter under the apple trees and allowed her the freedom of the garden, where she quickly became a firm favourite.

As she'd grown she'd moved to a shelter in the fields, where she'd remained friendly, always ready to come when called and welcoming all visitors with happy grunts and squeals.

In the years we'd had her, Sally had grown into a good breeder. The birth of her first litter had been a family event. We had all gathered to watch and had been amazed at how seemingly easy the delivery process was.

Rather than agonising like some animals, Sally had lain stretched out in the straw in a trancelike state while tiny piglets popped out like peas from a pod. It had been little short of miraculous the way each piglet had got shakily to its feet, then wobbled its way to its mother's teats where it had immediately got on with the job of feeding itself. There had been no motherly licking or encouragement as with, say, sheep. The teats were simply a readily available source of milk and warmth to be used – or not – as the piglet saw fit.

This was, we learned, merely a matter of efficient childbirth.

Sally conserved her energy while delivering her children but once that was over her maternal instincts were powerful.

Over the years she'd had two more litters. In the weeks that followed the arrival of her offspring, Sally was always a protective and dutiful mother. At the slightest whisper in her ear from one of her piglets, she would flop on to her side and let her children suckle.

It hadn't been plain sailing with her, of course. Pigs are notoriously unfussy eaters and can let their greed get the better of them at times. On one occasion we found Sally in her pen choking, barely able to breathe.

Over the phone the vet told us it was probably something blocking her windpipe. The key thing was to keep Sally moving around in the hope that whatever was causing the obstruction would eventually become dislodged.

Sally was a firm favourite with all the family and everyone rallied round to make sure she kept on the move. This carried on for a couple of days, but with little change in Sally's condition. Then, on the third day, Sally's breathing was even worse and she seemed in real distress. This time we asked the vet to come out.

'There's only one thing for it,' he said, rolling up his sleeve. 'I'm going to have to see what's in there.'

I had my doubts about this. Sally had grown into a very large sow, and even though her temperament was extremely good, I knew it wasn't the easiest thing in the world to open a pig's mouth. With my help the vet managed to force her jaws apart, allowing Julie to look down Sally's throat with a torch.

'I can't see anything,' she reported, rather disappointed. 'But hold on a minute. Let me try something else.'

In an instant she had produced a long piece of hosepipe, which she then proceeded to gently feed down Sally's throat. A few moments later the pipe was withdrawn again and Sally started coughing. As she retched away, what should pop out but a large piece of bone. She'd probably stolen it from one of the dogs, we concluded.

If I'd learned one thing about pigs over the years, it was that they are intelligent animals. Sally was no exception; she was always very quick on the uptake. She never ate a dog's bone again.

As the golden sun sank further into the west, the sound of a minibus pulling up outside the centre signalled the first arrival of the evening.

At the gate, I greeted the group's leader and a dozen or so neatly uniformed young girls. Their ages ranged from around nine to twelve, and they were terribly polite. I ushered them into the office where I was to give the talk.

Talking about myself was not something that came naturally to me. So instead I began by giving the girls a potted history of the centre and the kind of work we did there. I rattled through the stories of a few of our recent patients, then recalled some of the most memorable stories from the past, like those of Bracken the pony, Harry the dingo and Snip, the squirrel who had been so reluctant to go back to his real home. The young girls seemed interested enough, particularly when the subject of the story was a cute, fluffy creature they could relate to. But I could sense the restlessness, especially among the younger ones.

'So, who'd like to go out to the sanctuary and see some of the animals?' I asked after about ten minutes. Unsurprisingly, a sea of hands went up in the air. 'Right, then, off we go,' I said.

I took the girls around the cattery first. The sight of ten or so fluffy orphans had the usual effect. The girls were soon on their knees, stroking and fussing over their favourite felines. It took a gentle order from Brown Owl to get them to move on to the large aviaries.

There was a peacock and a pheasant in there at the time. Odin, too, was still there, as mischievous as ever. When one of the girls strayed a little too close to his cage, he suddenly stuck out his beak.

'Watch that one, he's a devil,' I said, before regaling them with various tales from the raven's past. The story of how he had tricked Klair by playing possum produced the biggest laugh of the evening.

'Right, who would like to see the guinea pigs and rabbits?' I asked as we'd completed our tour of the cages in the new centre.

Again the enthusiasm was considerable, so I marched the group through the gates leading to the yard, heading towards the field shelter behind the house.

It was a decision I was soon to regret.

To get to the shelter, we had to walk through the yard. To my horror, I saw that it was occupied by two very large pigs. They were locked together in what can only be described as the full throes of passion.

In organising this evening for the Brownies, this was the one thing I'd been concerned about. So I'd spoken to the pig farmer in advance of his visit and left clear instructions. During the period when I was due to be in the office, delivering my talk, he was to reverse his special pig transporter through the yard, then let it into the fields behind the house where Julie had put Sally for the evening. That way, I'd figured, the two pigs could get on with what came naturally far away from the gaze of these impressionable young girls.

My plans had clearly backfired, however. I would have to wait to find out what precisely had gone wrong. My priority now was to save the girls' blushes.

'Oh, dear. Sorry, you weren't supposed to see that,' I said, trying to shoo the girls through the yard as quickly as possible.

221

There was no way they could fail to be fascinated by the rutting pigs, however. Three or four of them were fixed to the spot, their jaws wide open as they watched the two hefty animals writhing around together. After a while the boar decided he'd completed what he'd come to achieve this evening and slumped, exhausted on Sally's back, leaving her to bear his considerable weight.

The questions started coming quick and fast.

'Mr Harper, what are they doing?'

'Mr Harper, why were those pigs panting like that?'

'Why is that pig sleeping on top of the other one?'

I didn't really know what to do, so I turned to their Brown Owl. 'I think it's best if Brown Owl explains that to you,' I said, passing the buck. The look she flashed me spoke volumes.

It was another ten minutes or so before I was able to usher the Brownies back into their minibus and wave them off. No sooner had they gone than I found the pig farmer having a nap in his Land Rover.

'What on earth happened there?' I asked him.

'It was your sow that started it.' He shrugged and went on to explain how when he'd arrived in the yard, Sally had burst through a gate and presented herself immediately to his boar. 'She was waiting for him.'

'But how the heck did she get there?' I asked him, to be greeted with nothing more than another shrug. 'She would have had to walk around half a dozen fields and lift off the five-bar gates from their drop-down hinges in every one of them,' I went on.

'Sows get very worked up if they know there's a boar coming,' he said eventually. 'What was my boy to do? I just let them get on with it.'

I couldn't really make much of a complaint. I shouldn't have double-booked the two events for the night. It was my fault.

By the time I saw the pig farmer on his way, the last sliver of sunlight was disappearing over the horizon and the first stars were out.

'What's got into you?' Julie asked, when I arrived in the kitchen and slumped into a chair.

When I explained what had happened she burst into fits of laughter I thought would never cease.

'You should have charged those Brownies,' she said, eventually suppressing her mirth.

'What do you mean?' I said.

'Well, they didn't just get a talk on the RSPCA. They got a free biology lesson as well.'

CHAPTER NINETEEN
'It Takes All Sorts'

With the RSPCA's plans now transformed into reality, a highly professional and rather impressive set-up had taken shape at Ferndale by the late 1980s. The offices, kennels, catteries and aviaries were hives of activity from dawn to dusk.

The days when Annie and Mrs K had been able to run the place together had long gone. Indeed, so had Annie, who had moved on to another career. She had been replaced by three other assistants, Vicky, Karen and Sue, who had been so upset by the loss of our greenfinches. The other important member of the team was Liz, a lady who had started as a volunteer but had become a real godsend for Julie and me. At the drop of a hat she would look after the farm for us if we were called away or decided to take a brief holiday.

The new, expanded office had also become the communications centre for all of Cornwall and was taking seventy calls a day. To cope with this, we had two telephonists, Pauline and Carol, working on a rota basis. They also helped out with the animals when they had time.

The centre's office provided a base for the county's team of RSPCA inspectors. This meant the place could be rather overcrowded at times, particularly when inspectors were checking in animals or writing up their reports.

The last piece in the jigsaw had been to recruit a permanent salaried warden to oversee the centre's operations on a day-to-day basis. The RSPCA hadn't had to look too far afield to find him. He was another local. In fact, he was about as local as you could get. Me.

The financial landscape had changed for the RSPCA and they were able to pay a proper full-time salary. I'd accepted the job the minute it was offered to me. It made complete sense. Returning briefly to the Post Office had reminded me how much I disliked 5 a.m. starts.

The only sadness about all the changes that had taken place was that the man who had made them largely possible wasn't around to see them. In March 1983 I'd arrived home from work one morning to discover Julie in floods of tears.

'Something awful's happened,' she had said between sobs. 'Ralph's died.'

The news had hit me like a thunderbolt. In truth I could hardly believe it. Since he'd first ridden to our rescue at the Rosery, twenty years or so earlier, Ralph Gardner had been our guide, our mentor and our friend. Personally speaking, I'd learned to value his advice above perhaps that of anyone I'd met. He had always been around to provide help, and had been quick to put us back on track if we had become too sentimental or enthusiastic, as perhaps we did now and again. Ralph had been, quite literally, a tower of strength, a father figure.

What made his loss all the more tragic was that he had been weeks away from retirement. He had died from a massive heart attack after attending a meeting in London.

Over the days following his death, the obituaries were generous, acknowledging his understanding and sympathy for the Cornish farm industry in particular. He was also remembered as the man who was responsible for overseeing the massive rescue operation that followed the *Torrey Canyon* disaster.

Ralph's replacement as chief inspector, Les Sutton, was a very different character. Whereas Ralph was very down to earth, someone who didn't suffer fools, Les was a softer character. That didn't mean he wasn't effective, though. We formed a good working relationship, which was just as well given the cramped conditions at the centre's office, which became his base too.

Life as a warden had some similarities to the old job at the Post Office. I still had a uniform, of sorts, consisting of navy-blue trousers and pullover, blue shirt and black tie, all of which were usually covered with a set of overalls. Another similarity was that the local RSPCA branch had decided that I needed a van to get on with my various responsibilities. There wasn't a specialist animal-collection officer, so a lot of the pickups were carried out by me. The white van had come complete with a pair of magnetic RSPCA logos attached to the side. There were also two smaller signs, with the word 'Warden' on them. I was rather proud of these. Unfortunately, on my second call-out the warden stickers were stolen, never to be recovered or replaced.

As with the Post Office job, the days were always full. I'd start around eight, when I'd make an inspection of the animals and help the assistants with the cleaning and exercising of the dogs. I'd then try and plan my day according to what was needed.

Some days I might need to take animals to the vet, others I might need to pick up various foodstuffs or check out release sites. Most days I tried to be available for a couple of hours, usually between 11 a.m. and 1 p.m., to deal with the phone messages that had arrived earlier in the morning to interview members of the public who were prospective adoptees.

This always had to be a flexible arrangement, however. The nature of an RSPCA warden's job is such that he has to be ready at any time of the night or day to assist an inspector who needs help with animal-related problems. From the beginning, there was no shortage of these.

If all was calm, my afternoons were usually devoted to picking up animals that had been delivered to the vet's in the morning to be neutered or spayed. If not, I would take more phone calls and interview more adoptees.

Part of my responsibility lay in forging links with the local community, so the odd afternoon involved visits to schools, women's institutes and other groups to give talks on the work of the centre and the inspectorate in general. During the summer and autumn visits to the centre during the evenings were arranged for adult societies and groups of Cubs, Brownies, Scouts and Guides – though I made sure I never gave another free biology lesson! They would all be given a tour of the centre, ending up with tea and biscuits in the office, when I would answer questions. All this could sometimes go on for hours.

Once a fortnight I'd travel to BBC Radio Cornwall, where the RSPCA had a regular fifteen-minute slot to talk about animal issues and problems. I would alternate with Les Sutton in these duties. We spoke about any interesting happenings within the society locally, and usually mentioned dogs, cats or other animals that we had waiting for homes. It proved a very useful outlet and we placed many animals as a result of the broadcast.

Although in theory I finished work at 5 p.m., there were very few days when Julie could expect me in for my meal before about 6 p.m. If my years working with animals had taught me anything, it was that there is always another job to do.

To Julie's occasional frustration, the fact that I was in the house didn't always mean I was off duty either. Living next door to the centre had many compensations, but it also had its downside in that people would often arrive at our door during the evening, when the centre was closed.

On numerous occasions people turned up with a young or injured bird, a fox cub or an unwanted dog or cat. We got used to disturbed meals, but we did eventually have to go ex-directory with our phone in order to get a bit of peace.

The straw that broke the camel's back came when a lady phoned at 11 p.m. one evening to ask if she could bring her dog the next day to have its claws clipped. Julie didn't mince her words in telling her she had the wrong number! My new role as warden opened my eyes to the funnier side of life too. On an almost daily basis I came across people whose eccentricities proved that old saying 'It takes all sorts.'

One morning, for instance, I got a call asking me to visit a man who, the caller claimed, was abusing his goats terribly. Such reports were far from uncommon. Goats are one of the most abused of our domestic animals. Many are kept under the most unsuitable conditions for use as scrub-clearers, often by people who have no idea of the creatures' needs, content to allow the animals to spend their entire lives at the end of a chain or rope, out in all weathers, often with no adequate shelter.

Goats hate the cold and wet, for although they grow quite thick coats, they feel the cold far more than sheep and quickly lose condition if they are tethered out of doors during the winter.

During my years with the RSPCA we received countless phone calls concerning goats. Some involved animals that had strangled themselves, having jumped over a wall or hedge while tethered; others related to starving goats, expected to be able to survive on the scantiest of vegetable matter, on chains that were seldom moved; some reports were simply of straying goats that had been turned loose and abandoned by their owners, who could no longer be bothered with them. So it can be seen that there was a pretty constant stream of goats coming through the RSPCA centre in need of treatment and, later, rehoming.

I knew I had to take this particular call seriously and, having called an inspector, headed off with him in the van as soon as possible.

The address I'd been given turned out to be a terraced cottage in a small village near Truro. It looked a bit run-down. There was no sign of a goat in the small garden at the front, so the inspector knocked at the door. When the door eventually opened, it revealed an elderly and extremely unkempt man, dressed only in a vest and trousers. I was struck by an overpowering smell that I recognised immediately.

Male billy goats are not the sweetest-smelling of animals, to put it mildly. This may well be connected with their rather unpleasant habit of urinating on to the hair of their bellies to attract female, or nanny, goats. The pungent aroma may be a turn-on for the girl goats, but it is an offence to the human nose.

After introducing himself, the inspector asked if he could see the goat, and, even though he already had a pretty good idea, tentatively enquired as to where it was kept.

'Oh,' the old fellow said in a rich Cornish accent, ''e do live in the 'ouse with me.'

That was blatantly obvious the moment we stepped inside. There were just two rooms downstairs and both had goat droppings thickly spread over the floor.

The goat had been dining well. The wall, up to the height of about six feet, had been completely stripped of wallpaper, and two-thirds of the curtains had been eaten away. Even the wood surrounding the windows had been chewed to pieces.

We discovered the culprit, a large white billy goat, in a corner of the living room calmly chewing mouthfuls of hay!

The inspector and I had seen enough already. Yes, the stench was overpowering and the damage to the property painfully obvious, yet the truth of the matter was, the old fellow and his goat companion were happy with each other's company. There was no hint of abuse or mistreatment of any kind. Indeed it was obvious the goat ate well. He was literally eating his keeper out of house and home!

We bade our farewells and concluded that the complaint was more about the terrible smell than anything else. If the neighbour wanted to complain to the council about that, it was up to him. The RSPCA had no business here.

As we headed back to the centre, the inspector and I kept the windows of the van wide open. After a quarter of an hour in that house, the clean Cornish air smelled sweeter than ever.

The old goat keeper was certainly an eccentric character, but some time later I met another fan of the animal that put even him in the shade.

A huge, large-horned, heavily coated billy goat had been found wandering the lanes a few miles away from Ferndale.

No one had come forward to claim him, so he had remained in our compound for many weeks, much to the displeasure of the staff, who were greeted at feeding times by the rather intimidating sight of the billy with his head lowered and his fearsome-looking horns poised to charge at them.

We had tried all the usual channels to rehome the goat, but with no luck. In the end it was an announcement on Radio Cornwall that did the trick. Shortly after an appeal for a home for the goat had been broadcast, a rather grand-looking Land Rover drew up on the centre forecourt and, from the back seat, out stepped an even grander-looking lady.

'Good morning,' she announced in an impeccable accent. 'I'm enquiring about the goat Radio Cornwall advertised as needing a home.'

'Certainly, madam,' I said, resisting the temptation to bow as I did so. 'Wait a moment.'

I found the billy goat eating out in the pasture. I managed to clip a dog lead on to his collar and bring him into the yard for her ladyship's inspection.

Her reaction was immediate – and unforgettable.

'Oh, the darling,' she said. 'My nannies are going to love you!' She then promptly threw her arms round the goat's neck and hugged him.

By now I'd been joined by a few other members of staff. We all stood there speechless, not quite believing what we were seeing.

Within a few minutes the formalities of the adoption procedure had been completed and the Land Rover was heading off once more with the chauffeur at the wheel and his employer sitting in the back with her arms still wrapped round her smelly new animal.

'Goodness gracious me, you know what they say,' I said to Vicky, heading back to the office.

'I know, Rex,' she said, interrupting me. 'It takes all sorts.' If goats were unlikely pets, then pigs were even less obvious candidates, yet in the 1980s, with the arrival of the Vietnamese pot-bellied pig, they became the height of fashion – and the occasional bane of my life.

These small, black members of the porcine family roam around the villages in their native Vietnam eating anything that comes their way. In the Far East, they are taken for granted, left to feed until they are big enough to make a decent cut of pork. For some unfathomable reason, however, the pigs' turned-up snub noses, short legs, fat-rolled flanks and plump pot bellies had endeared them to people in America and here in the UK.

Like all pigs, they are highly intelligent, so their popularity was helped by the fact they are relatively easy to house-train, at least when they are young. The problems come when the pig grows up, becoming a single-minded adult in the process. As many owners around the country quickly discovered, it is one thing to have a delightful piglet running around the house and quite another to have a stubborn adult that is remarkably solid and difficult to move around when it doesn't want to.

No sooner had the fashion spread its way down to Cornwall than the RSPCA centre had begun to pick up frequent calls from people who had misguidedly taken on these pigs. I'd personally collected a group of them from the most unlikely locations, including a couple of upstairs flats.

The call I got one day from a house in Truro led to the most memorable intervention by far. It came from the occupant of a house on a council estate.

'You'd better come and get our pigs,' she said. 'They're eating the estate up.'

She wasn't exaggerating. I arrived to discover a scene of complete carnage.

The caller, mother to a young family, had initially bought a pair of pot-bellied piglets. They'd been housed in a nice pen with a shed for shelter and had been popular not just with her children but the entire neighbourhood.

But things had changed.

As they'd matured, the two pigs had begun digging up the soil in the garden, turning the patch of grass into a mudbath. The pigs had also started rubbing themselves vigorously against the neighbouring fences, rendering them so unstable they eventually collapsed. This had resulted in their moving into the neighbours' gardens and digging them up too. They had also consumed the entire contents of one neighbour's vegetable patch.

Needless to say, the welcome mat had been well and truly removed. Complaints had been made to the council, but the pigs' owner hadn't taken any notice.

By now things had escalated yet further. The pigs had given birth to a litter of five piglets, who had joined them in the garden!

I looked out over a series of back gardens that looked like a very messy allotment. Fences were strewn everywhere, and large chunks of earth had been excavated as if by a giant mole. Worst of all, the air was thick with the rather pungent aroma of pot-bellied pig manure. I could see why the neighbours had got the council to force the owners to call us in.

Pigs are not the easiest of animals to handle or capture, mainly because their smooth bodies mean there is very little you can cling on to. Even if you are lucky enough to grab an ear, the sheer bulk of the pig makes it almost impossible to maintain a grip. Fortunately, however, I'd been taught well by the countrymen with whom I had shared my childhood and I relied on a tried-and-trusted technique for rounding them up. A dustbin.

If a pig can see where it is going, then it will only head where it wants. With its head covered, though, it loses all sense of direction and becomes quite docile. You can then guide it wherever *you* like.

I got a few odd looks when I asked for a plastic dustbin, but one soon materialised. I put it over the elder pot-bellied pig and led it backwards towards the van. Once it was safely installed, I repeated the process with its mate, then rounded the piglets up by hand. I then left the neighbourhood to – literally – patch things up.

It didn't take long to find new homes for the pigs. A few phone calls quickly located some farm parks that were interested in acquiring the pigs and their offspring. They were soon settling into slightly more appropriate surroundings.

CHAPTER TWENTY
The House of Horrors

It was the smell that hit me first. As I walked through the back door of the cottage into a dark passageway, the stale, sour stench filled my nostrils. It was so overwhelming it made my eyes water. It didn't take long to work out where it was coming from. As I passed through the back door, I sensed I was sloshing my way through what felt like a few inches of water.

'Where's all this water coming from? Is there a burst main here or something?' I asked Mike, the inspector I'd been asked to accompany today, seeing in the gloom that my gumboots were ankle-deep.

'I wish it was water, Rex,' Mike replied. 'It's urine. The

toilet's blocked and the place is swimming in it.' As we made our way forward I had a feeling even more grim surprises lay in store.

I'd been slightly taken aback when I'd been asked to join Mike at this house in Redruth. I knew of it a little. It was a cottage at the end of a terrace on the edge of town. It sold fresh eggs and poultry and had done so for many years. No one had complained about the place before, but a few days ago the RSPCA had got a call from the owner, an elderly man who said both he and his wife had been taken ill and were no longer living there. He had asked that his hens be taken away.

Since then, someone had made a preliminary visit. He had wasted no time in summoning not just two RSPCA officers but also the police and a team of pest-control experts. As Mike and I walked into the living room at the front of the house, it was clear everyone had been surprised by what they'd discovered.

A policeman and two pest-control experts were engaged in quiet conversation, each of them shaking their heads ruefully. Mike and I were soon mirroring their expressions. Looking around the room, it seemed impossible that anyone could have sat, let alone lived in this place. Everywhere there were piles of rotting furniture and stained, peeling wallpaper. Incongruously, right in the middle of this chaos stood a brand-new television set, its large screen gleaming amid the squalor of the rest of the room.

Out of the corner of my eye, I thought for a moment I saw a dead rat.

'Yes, that is what you think it is,' said one of the pest-control men. 'And there are plenty more where that one came from, so watch out.'

Mike and I knew the rats were their concern, not ours. We

had to locate the chickens, although it was soon clear they were not the only animals in residence here.

In one corner of the living room, assorted rubbish was piled high. I moved to see if there was anything lurking behind. Almost at once three lean and very frightened cats emerged from behind an old sideboard. There was no time to even attempt to capture them. Leaping over the piles of rubble, they shot out of the door and vanished upstairs.

'We'll find them later,' I said to Mike. 'Let's see what's in the kitchen.'

A similarly disgusting scene greeted us there. More dead rats lay around, this time in the midst of a pile of grime-encrusted empty milk bottles and an assortment of plastic items. Scanning the room, I saw a blackened electric cooker, its wires dangling, and an incredibly filthy kitchen table, piled high with dirty crockery. There were, however, no animals, unless you counted the large number of flies that buzzed about our heads and darkened the small windowpanes.

'Shall we try upstairs?' I said to Mike, slightly nervously. 'It might smell a bit better up there.'

But no sooner had we set foot on the bare wooden staircase than it became obvious that the upper part of the cottage was in an even worse state of repair than downstairs. At some stage the ceilings had collapsed, leaving the roof trusses exposed. Above that, it was clear that the slates had moved or were missing. The roof timbers were covered in damp patches. I was standing on the landing surrounded by fallen plaster, trying to imagine what it must have been like to live here on a cold, Cornish winter's night with the wind whistling and the rain falling, when I saw that we were being watched.

Perched on the timbers surveying us with frightened eyes were ten or more cats. When I pointed them out to Mike, they panicked. The slim, wary creatures soon scurried along the rafters back into the darker recesses of the attic. Again I resolved to deal with them later.

On either side of the small landing, two closed doors suggested bedrooms. We headed through the left-hand door and stepped into another scene from a horror film.

Everything in the room was a putrid black: the walls, the floor, the rotting chairs and, in the middle of it all, a double bed, covered with an indescribable assortment of filthy bedclothes. Once more the sour smell of the room was nauseating.

I spotted a small crack in a wardrobe door, perhaps wide enough for an animal to have squeezed through.

'Let's see if one of those cats crept in there,' I said to Mike.

What met our eyes once the door was pulled open took us both by surprise. There, perched on a pile of old clothes that had been scraped together to make a rough nest, was a hen sitting on a clutch of eggs.

'Fresh eggs for sale,' I muttered to myself, shuddering at the very thought.

Before we could explore the room further we were both distracted by the noise of what sounded like the scuffling and scraping of moving animals coming from the other bedroom. Mike pushed open the door to reveal a scene that will for ever be imprinted on my memory.

The room was about twelve feet square and devoid of any furniture. The floor was completely covered with a thick layer of poultry droppings, which, over a long period of time had dried out and caked into a thick crust, several inches deep and more or less flat, but with a small dark hole in its surface, right in the middle of the room.

Strutting towards us across this mess were twelve large, hungry-looking cockerels. They were, it has to be said, in a much better condition than you would have expected them to be. They had obviously been fed quite recently and from their demeanour expected to be fed again.

I spotted an old plastic dustbin containing some grain and dished out a few handfuls. The cockerels were soon dashing around pecking at the food.

They were not alone for long. The bird that emerged out of the dark hole in the middle of the floor was small and pale. It was closely followed by another similar-looking bird. They were pullets, female chickens.

No sooner had they begun pecking at the grain, however, than the twelve cockerels completely enveloped the two new-comers in a flapping, cackling frenzy, raising clouds of dust from the floor. After several seconds the rough and tumble subsided, the cockerels resumed their meal and the dust cloud settled. The two pale birds had vanished.

The only possible hiding place was the hole in the floor. Sure enough, on closer inspection, it turned out to be a small cardboard box, entirely submerged beneath a thick coating of droppings so that it had become virtually a cave below floor level.

Inside the box, squashed together, were ten pullets, so tightly packed that they had difficulty in moving at all. They were almost completely devoid of feathers and were so thin they were mere skeletons.

I marvelled that they had survived; certainly another few days and they would have been dead. Just how long the birds had been forced to endure this terrible existence was not clear. My guess was that the cockerels and the pullets had been put in the room as young stock and had probably coexisted quite happily until the cockerels became sexually mature. At that point they would have begun sexually attacking the pullets. The pullets had obviously taken refuge in their tiny sanctuary. Little wonder they had remained there starving. I imagined that as soon as one ventured out, it would immediately be attacked and raped by the cockerels.

Mike and I were, I think, both in a state of mild shock. It took us a moment to grasp the enormity of what we had discovered. We quickly gathered ourselves, however. We had both seen enough and began planning the hens' removal.

Within an hour or so, we'd got the pullets out and into the back of the van. They drank the water they were offered with all the relish of a man arriving at an oasis after a week in the desert. I could see that, with care, they would make a good recovery. They would, in time, forget the hellhole in which they had been incarcerated.

The following day we returned to collect the cockerels, who also looked likely to recover and forget about their confinement. I, however, knew I wouldn't. I had seen enough in my years taking in waifs and strays to know that humans were more than capable of treating animals with neglect and cruelty, but when I'd agreed to become a warden, I hadn't quite expected to see scenes such as this.

It was beyond anything I had ever encountered. It left me feeling shaken and depressed for days.

CHAPTER TWENTY-ONE

Expect the Unexpected

Whenen Julie announced someone from the lifeguard hut at Perranporth Beach was on the phone for me, I immediately assumed they were calling about an injured seabird or perhaps a large beached fish. Basking sharks and even whales had come to grief and been stranded along the Cornish coast in the past.

So when the caller revealed that some local children had found a badger trapped in a cave at the water's edge I didn't quite believe what I was hearing.

'I'm sorry, did you say a badger?' I stammered. 'What on earth is a badger doing down on the beach?'

It was a hot summer afternoon at the height of the tourist

season, and the last thing I wanted to do was fight my way on to a crowded beach. But I knew immediately this was a potentially dangerous situation and I had no choice but to head down there. I asked Karen, one of the centre's assistants, to give me a hand and we started getting the van ready.

Badgers were no strangers to us. They were frequent visitors to the centre, almost always as the victims of accidents. I had no doubt why badgers got themselves into trouble so regularly. As the countryside's top predators, they have no enemies, apart from man, that is. As a result, they have a rather blasé approach to life and will take ridiculous and foolhardy risks. They will, for instance, cross busy roads with little or no regard for traffic. At the centre we had taken in a number of badgers that had been found at the roadside, having been mown down by a passing car or lorry.

They would also jump into situations without thinking. We had cared for a number of badgers that had been found in empty swimming pools. They had usually jumped in in search of worms, then been unable to climb back out again. Badgers also get themselves caught in wire snares that have been set to catch rabbits. I knew from my experience at the centre and as a teenager catching rabbits that releasing badgers from those could be quite a challenge. Badgers tend to make a tremendous effort to break free, sometimes tangling themselves up in knots and cutting their necks badly on the nooses. We had had badgers brought in with really deep cuts that had taken weeks to heal properly.

On the whole they were good patients. Given a secure, secluded cage or pen, badgers settle down in confinement pretty well. But I knew from long experience that they could be extremely dangerous too, especially if not handled correctly, as a young vet had once found out when helping

244

Julie transfer a badger from a carrying box to an indoor pen. As they'd got ready to make the switch, Julie had repeatedly warned the vet to put on a pair of thick gloves or gauntlets. But the vet had seen the badger curled up in an innocent-looking ball, as they tend to do when they are worried, and had ignored her advice. No sooner had he reached into the box and grabbed the badger by the scruff of the neck than it had uncurled itself with lightning speed and sunk its teeth into his hand.

Believe me, it is not easy to get a badger to release its grip. It was only after a struggle and quite a lot of bloodletting on the part of the vet that the badger's teeth had been extricated from his hand. He had certainly learned a lesson he would never forget.

As we packed the van this afternoon, Karen and I made sure that among the equipment we took with us we each had a pair of protective gloves. It took us only a few minutes to reach the seafront at Perranporth. Taking advantage of the RSPCA insignia on the sides of the van, I drove across the sands to the lifeguard's hut. We had to pick our way across carefully. The whole beach was packed with people, sweltering in the heat. Worryingly, many of them were heading towards the end of the beach where the cave containing the badger was situated.

As Karen and I climbed out of the van and followed the throng, we could hear people calling to each other, 'There's a badger in a cave up here. Let's go and have a look.'

I just hoped that we had arrived in time to prevent someone getting injured. If the badger was approached too closely, it would feel threatened and attack. I was particularly worried that a child, lacking in fear and common sense, might go up and try to stroke the animal. The consequences in that situation did not bear thinking about.

When at last we arrived at the cave, crowds of children and adults had gathered outside the entrance. A few braver souls had gone inside and were standing within just a few feet of the badger, who I discovered was snarling at them from its position on a ledge, four or five feet up on the back wall.

I breathed a sigh of relief that we had arrived in time. No one had attempted to do anything silly. I asked the people to leave the cave, which, amazingly, they did without question. I followed them out into the sunshine and explained to the still thickening crowd the dangers involved where cornered badgers were concerned. I then told them what I was going to do to rescue this one.

We had brought a carrying cage and a 'grasper', an adjustable wire noose running through a long metal handle, which we used when savage or difficult animals had to be caught. I was going to slip this over the badger's neck, then transfer it to the cage. I left Karen to talk to the crowd and answer their questions and went back into the cave alone. I found the badger rolled up in that familiar ball-like position, effectively pretending he wasn't there.

'Come on, old lad, let's get you out of here,' I said, getting myself ready.

Speed was going to be of the essence. The actual procedure was, hopefully, going to take mere seconds. But as with all jobs of this kind, the key thing was preparation. Here, I had to make sure I was standing in a good position and that I could maintain my balance as I transferred the badger to the cage.

Badgers aren't the lightest of animals. This one looked to be fairly large and probably weighed in excess of four stones. I knew he was also going to struggle, so once the noose was attached, I was going to have to move quickly and efficiently in swinging it down and into the cage.

I took up a position below the badger and placed the cage to the side, with its gate open ready. I then extended the four-foot long 'grasper' slowly up towards the badger and gently touched him on his nose. Immediately the head emerged and the badger snarled at the object that had disturbed him. With a quick flick of the wrists, I slipped the noose over his head and swung him down off the ledge. As I'd anticipated, he flailed around wildly, but fortunately I managed to get him down on to the sand and into the cage in one smooth movement. I shut the door, then flicked the quick-release mechanism to release the noose.

There, job done, I said to myself, relieved it had gone well.

Inside the cage, the badger immediately resumed his curled-up position. As I carried the cage and its occupant out into the bright sunshine, the crowd at the cave entrance seemed delighted that all was well, and milled around trying to get a closer look.

Sensing the badger really didn't appreciate this kind of attention, I quickly put the cage in the back of the van and drove back to the RSPCA centre, where Karen and I performed a quick check on him. Fortunately, he seemed to have emerged from the experience unscathed. There were no signs of cuts or bruises of any kind.

It was almost dusk before Karen and I released him. As the sun began to set out on the horizon, we took him back down to the beach, this time on the dunes above the sands. I flipped open the cage and he immediately walked out. We watched him trundle off into the glow-worm-spangled marram grass, none the worse for his adventure but having provided no clues as to how he'd got himself stuck in the cave in the first place.

I'd been thinking about it ever since I'd got the call from the lifeguards earlier in the afternoon. The only explanation that made any sense to me was that he had been foraging on the shore at night when perhaps something had scared him so he had taken refuge in the cave. When day broke, he was probably too scared to venture out into the daylight, especially with the sound of people and dogs on the beach, which began almost at daybreak. He had stayed there until we'd come along to rescue him.

If it was frustrating not knowing exactly what had led the badger there, it was at least pleasing to think we had safely extricated the frightened animal from this situation.

As the centre's operations expanded more and more, I was learning to take odd episodes like this in my stride. 'Expect the unexpected' had almost become my motto.

A few weeks before the incident with the badger, for instance, just as we were about to turn in for bed one night, a middle-aged man had turned up on our doorstep looking like he'd seen a ghost.

'Something jumped into my car,' he said, his voice wavering a little. 'I haven't got a bloody clue what it is. Could you come and take it?'

As I grabbed a torch and some wellingtons, the chap explained that he'd been driving through a local village when he'd noticed what at first looked like a strange breed of dog trotting along the pavement. Intrigued, he'd stopped his car and opened his passenger door to have a closer look.

To his amazement and mild horror, the animal had approached him, then calmly jumped in and sat down alongside him. All his attempts to move the creature had failed. He had driven over to us immediately.

I was intrigued as to what he might have found. As I opened the door of the car and stared in, I was initially as flummoxed as the driver. The creature had a long, low-slung body and a tapering tail. Its most striking feature, however, was its long, very flexible nose, which it was quivering almost constantly, as if sniffing the air for something to eat.

'Well, I can tell you one thing,' I said, inspecting the creature closely. 'It's definitely not a dog.'

It didn't look like it was aggressive, so I carefully scooped it up and carried it into the office to get a better look.

Something made me suspect it was a jungle creature, probably from a hot climate. After a few moments a thought popped into my head.

'I wonder whether this might be a coatimundi,' I said, heading for the reference books we kept in the office.

Sure enough, in an encyclopaedia of animals, I found a photograph of a creature exactly like this one. It was a coatimundi, a native of the South American jungles.

In the wild, coatis spend much of their time on the forest floor snuffling through the leaf litter and eating everything from insects and scorpions to fallen fruit. This one seemed very tame and had clearly been used to human company, which immediately made me suspect it had escaped from a zoo or wildlife park of some kind.

The motorist was pleased to know the identity of his mysterious hitch-hiker and headed off, doubtless to wake up his wife and regale her with the story of his strange evening. I put the coati into the field shelter and turned in for the night.

It didn't take long the following morning for everyone at the centre to come up with a name for our new inmate. Coatis exude a pungent smell. He was soon being called Stinky.

Stinky quickly became a firm favourite with the centre's staff. We checked him out medically and he seemed to be in fine fettle. I had good contacts within the area's zoological circles. While getting advice from one of them about how to handle and feed Stinky, I learned that a pair of coatis had been sold by a local pet shop a couple of years earlier. This could well have been one of them.

We knew we couldn't keep him for long, so began a search for a suitable permanent home. We discovered that there was a small community of coatis at the Exmoor Wildlife Park in Devon. A couple of weeks after his dramatic arrival he was on his way to rejoin his own kind.

The coatimundi was one of many animals that were testing our knowledge and resourcefulness to the full. A few months before Stinky's arrival we'd had a racoon.

A small-dog-sized animal with a thick grizzled coat, bushy, black-ringed tail and a sharp, pointed face, the racoon is a distant cousin of the coatimundi. The black markings it has around its eyes make it look like it's wearing a robber's mask, which was rather appropriate in this case.

This particular racoon had obviously escaped from a wildlife centre or a private collection. In the wild, racoons are highly adaptable creatures and can survive on anything from bird's eggs to shellfish. Ours had been making do on the contents of binbags and dustbins. Until he had been caught red-handed rummaging through the rubbish in an outhouse, it had been assumed a fox was at work.

The racoon is a delightful creature, although its cuddly, teddy-bear-like appearance is deceptive. It can be very unpredictable and needs really careful handling. Racoons have very dextrous front paws, which make them great climbers. We had learned quickly that ours needed to be enclosed at all times otherwise he would have been out of his cage and scavenging again.

Fortunately, we hadn't had to keep him for long. A zoo 'up country' agreed to take him so he could join an existing community of racoons there.

On the bird front, one of the most unusual patients we'd

had was a waxwing. It had collapsed in a local garden on a cold winter's day and been brought to us near death. Waxwings are seldom seen in Cornwall but can be driven here from further north when the weather turns cold. This bird had been thin and quite obviously suffering from hypothermia, so we had placed it in a heated hospital cage, where it eventually showed signs of recovery.

My biggest concern, however, had been what to feed it. Waxwings are berry eaters, but these are in short supply in winter, even in Cornwall's relatively mild climes. Fortunately, I had remembered reading somewhere that waxwings have a liking for the berries of a cultivated shrub, *Cotoneaster horizontalis*. I had then rung a local garden centre, who had supplied me with some cotoneaster branches, complete with a bountiful supply of berries. The waxwing had gobbled them up, and when the weather had improved a week and a half after his arrival, he had been fit enough to return to the wild.

I must admit I had felt rather proud as he flew away into the clear winter's sky in search of a warm place to wait for the spring.

'Where are you off to in such a hurry?' Julie shouted as she saw me running across the yard towards the van one morning.

'Off to catch the beast of Bodmin Moor,' I shouted back, with a wave and a wry grin. 'Again.'

For three days running I'd been receiving phone calls from a local husband and wife who claimed they'd witnessed a large bobcat rampaging around the countryside. According to the couple, the cat had been killing rabbits on a hillside opposite their home. On two occasions I'd already visited the place where they claimed to have seen the beast, but with no luck.

The husband's tone on the phone had been almost apologetic as he called for the third time this morning. 'I know you think I'm some sort of crank,' he said, 'but I know a big cat when I see one – and this is a really big cat.'

His nervousness at being thought a fool was understandable. Sightings of so-called big cats across the countryside are part of British folklore. Like the Loch Ness Monster, they have gripped the imagination of the general public, even though there is little hard evidence to support their existence.

Although I'd met many people who claimed to have seen a big cat over the years, I'd never seen any really positive proof they existed. Yes, there was little doubt cats like the puma and the lynx, both masters of camouflage and quite able to adapt to our winters, could very easily establish themselves in remote places, but I remained sceptical, mainly because of my own personal experience.

A few years earlier, for instance, we'd had a call from a man who swore he'd seen a black panther near an abandoned poultry farm. Julie and I had driven to the spot where the animal had allegedly been sighted, and had searched for clues. The area had admittedly been an ideal big-cat habitat, with thick cover and a small wood of aged Scots pine, bordering a stream. It had been raining and we had examined the mud on the stream banks for any sign of pawprints, but to no avail. We had also scanned the pine trees with binoculars, in case a cat was lying among the branches, but there had been nothing.

It had been a beautiful morning, and following a night of rain, the countryside had been colourful with new plant growth. This, coupled with the clean, fresh smell of the pines, had made us reluctant to leave the spot and return to work, so we had sat by the van and enjoyed a bit of stolen leisure, at the same time surveying the surrounding fields and woodland for any sign of a big cat.

After a couple of hours we had just been about to call it a day when a really huge black tomcat strolled out from the undergrowth and walked calmly towards the empty farm buildings. So much for the black panther – the menace was nothing more than an overfed moggy!

The 'videos' that people frequently claimed to have obtained of these big beasts only added to my doubts. I remember one in which what was described as an 'enormous black cat' was seen stalking through woodland and tall vegetation. The only problem was that at one stage the cat passed a duck pond. The Aylesbury ducks walking alongside it were just as big as the giant cat! The man who made the video didn't take kindly to my pointing this out. I heard later that he continued showing the film as evidence of his beast being real – minus the footage of the ducks.

Yet when it came down to it, I was in no doubt that most of the people who called in with sightings genuinely believed they had seen a big cat. This was certainly the case with the couple who had reported the bobcat seen killing rabbits outside their flat.

Unfortunately, the first time I had visited them they had told me I'd missed the beast by a matter of minutes. The bobcat had apparently made a kill and vanished back into the thick cover of gorse bushes on the hillside. To their embarrassment, the same thing had happened the second time. Today, as I put my foot down and headed there as fast as I could, I had a feeling it was going to be third time lucky.

The couple's flat was only a mile or so away from Ferndale, on the side of a steep valley, a mile or so from the coast. As I pulled up, however, the couple met me at the door looking distraught.

'You're not going to believe this, but it's happened again,' the wife said. 'One minute it was there sitting in the sun, the next it was gone. We really are sorry about this. You must think we are the worst kind of time-wasters.'

I laughed. 'Don't worry, I'm sure our luck will change one day.'

Rather than rushing off, I accepted an invitation to have a cup of tea. Inside the flat, I sat in an armchair near the window, overlooking the hillside opposite.

I had a couple of theories that explained the recent rise in sightings of strange creatures and shared them with the couple.

'A lot of this is down to the new Dangerous Wild Animals Act,' I explained. 'People now have to get a licence to keep an exotic animal. A lot of them simply can't be bothered to go through all the expense and red tape so they just let their creatures loose. I've heard of all sorts of animals being spotted. It wouldn't surprise me if someone lets a lion or a tiger loose one day, then we'll be in trouble.'

As we chatted I kept half an eye on the gorse-patched slopes in case anything unexpected happened. Sure enough, after just a few minutes I noticed several rabbits leaving the cover of the gorse to graze out on the grass. Then, suddenly, all the rabbits started rushing madly down the slope, as if they were being chased.

'Looks like there's something going on out there,' I said, putting my tea down and moving nearer the window for a better look.

The husband was soon standing at my side. I could sense his anticipation. Was this, at last, the moment he was going to be vindicated?

After another brief flurry of activity from the rabbits, a creature emerged from the overgrowth. It was a tawny orange cat and it was soon dashing down the hillside with strange, loping bounds.

'That's him, that's him,' the husband said excitedly, pointing at the feline form zigzagging its way down the hillside in pursuit of the rabbits that were now scattering in all directions.

The cat was obviously well used to hunting in this terrain and quickly overhauled the slowest of the rabbits. With a lightning blow it caught one in its claws. It then turned quickly, the rabbit held firmly in its mouth and disappeared back into the gorse.

The whole sequence had lasted less than ten seconds, but I'd had enough time to reach a few conclusions. The animal we'd been watching was a domestic cat. Yes, it was tail-less, but that could be explained by any number of factors. It might, for instance, have had a Manx ancestor or perhaps have met with an accident.

As for its hunting ability, well, this had been left totally unimpaired. It was possible, I thought, that it had been living wild for a long time and turned feral. Equally, however, it could be one of the many cats that lived a double life, purring away contentedly at home as if butter wouldn't melt in its mouth, then turning into a serial killer outdoors when its owner's back was turned.

'I'm terribly sorry to disappoint you,' I said, eventually turning to the couple. 'But I'm afraid it's a domestic cat. It's a big one, I'll grant you that. But nevertheless it's a normal household cat, not a bobcat.'

I could see from the expressions on their faces that the couple were let down. I wasn't certain they fully believed me either, so I went into more detail about the difference between this and an American bobcat.

'But what about the tail?' the husband asked. 'That's what made me think it was a bobcat.'

'He's just lost his rudder at some point,' I said. 'Given the way he chases other animals, I wouldn't be surprised if he's got himself into a few scrapes over the years.'

'Oh,' the wife said, looking even more crestfallen than her husband. 'I thought we might have solved the mystery of the Beast of Bodmin Moor. I had images of TV crews camping outside.'

'Sorry,' was all I could say.

CHAPTER TWENTY-TWO
Working the Dogs

As I headed home from a long walk with the dogs one Sunday morning there was no mistaking the onset of another autumn. Further down the valley towards the sea, most of the birds had headed off for warmer climes, leaving the mist-wreathed marshes still and eerily quiet. In the woods along the stream at the perimeter of our land, the dead trees were covered with parasol-shaped fungi. Everywhere the air was scented with the smell of damp earth and rotting leaves.

So the sound of a Land Rover crunching to a halt in the gravel outside the office resonated right across the fields. I arrived there to be greeted by a rather ruddy-looking old farmer. He was wearing a flat cap and overalls and was puffing on a pipe. Alongside him stood a small black-and-white Border collie.

'Afternoon,' he said. 'I was wondering if you would take in this 'ere dog.'

The collie looked perfectly well to me. It had kind eyes and an intelligent look.

'Why, what's wrong with her?' I said.

'Bought her in Wales at a sheepdog sale. Supposed to have been trained for work but she won't do a flippin' thing for me,' he said, with a disdainful look at the dog.

'What's her name?' I asked.

'Rose,' he replied.

I'd seen enough of the mistreatment meted out by some farmers to unwanted animals to know there was no way I could let the collie return home.

'All right, leave her with me and I'll try to find a good home for her,' I said.

No sooner had he handed over her lead than the farmer was fishing in his pockets. To my amazement, he produced a fifty-pound note, which he handed to me. 'Thanks very much. Put this in your funds,' he said, before swivelling on his heels and climbing back into the Land Rover.

'Well, well, well,' I said to our newest arrival. 'Wonders never cease.'

I had to finish some paperwork so kept Rose in the office with me for the rest of the afternoon. She didn't seem happy, however, and paced the office nervously. At one point she even tried to get out of a partly open window.

Unable to pacify her, I decided I'd better put her in the kennels. As I was about to head off, Julie appeared.

Julie has always had an uncanny knack of connecting with dogs, and so it proved again. The transformation was remarkable and immediate. Rose instantly calmed down and sat at Julie's feet. I'd seen dogs react to her in this way many times, but even by her standards this was out of the ordinary.

'So, what's wrong with this one?' Julie asked, as the dog nestled up alongside her.

'Can't work sheep apparently,' I said. 'Although I don't think I'd have wanted to work for her owner either.'

Julie gave Rose's neck a ruffle. 'I bet you're a perfectly good worker, aren't you?' she said. 'Come on, let's give you a try out.'

As it happened, Julie had been moving some of her sheep around the fields that morning. She was going to check on them anyway so took Rose with her. She kept the new arrival on a lead for safety's sake. She needn't have worried.

I went along for a walk and was glad I did, otherwise I wouldn't have believed what happened. The moment the sheep loomed into view Rose was off, instinctively nudging them into a tidy grouping. Julie was flabbergasted, as indeed was I.

'There's nothing wrong with that one,' I said.

'Nothing at all,' said Julie. 'I think I've got myself a sheepdog.'

From that moment on Rose and Julie were inseparable.

Rose showed her worth again the next morning. A neighbour had sold his herd of cattle and was having it collected. The cattle trucks were parked in the road with their ramps down as the cows were being loaded. We had popped along to give him a hand and Julie had brought her new dog with her.

All went well until a mature bull refused to go on to the ramp and headed off at speed up our quiet minor road towards the busy main road half a mile away.

On seeing this, Rose gave Julie a look as if to say, 'Shall I sort it out?' Julie understood her immediately and gave her the nod. She was soon haring off down the road in pursuit of the bull.

Rose had soon got herself into a position ahead of the bull, but the animal was reluctant to turn back. As Rose moved in closer, the bull lowered his head menacingly, but our new dog wasn't deterred; in fact the move had the opposite effect.

Rose suddenly surprised the bull by running in like lightning and giving him a quick nip on the nose. Completely put off his stride, the bull turned round in the lane and started trotting back towards the lorries, the little dog cajoling him along every step of the way.

'I don't believe what I've just seen,' I said to Julie.

She just stood there beaming. The welcome she gave Rose was fulsome.

Over the coming weeks and months Rose became Julie's right hand, helping her move all her domestic animals around the farm. She was as adept at steering poultry where she wanted them as she was at herding cattle and sheep. She was the perfect working dog, in fact.

Neither of us could work out why she hadn't done this for her previous owner. Perhaps he hadn't had the patience. Or perhaps, as Julie suggested, his voice had been too harsh and Rose responded better to a softer, female tone. Whatever the reason, we were grateful she'd got herself sacked from her previous job. She was one of the best employees we'd had yet.

Animals are a little like London buses. You wait ages for a particular species to come along, then before you know it there are two or three of them heading your way. So it proved with Border collies. Within weeks of Rose arriving, two more turned up. This time they were unwanted pups, the last two of a large litter. They were ten weeks old, smallish in size but in good condition.

Along with German shepherds, collies are a breed I admire hugely. I thought I might keep one for myself so I decided to test them immediately. I took both pups to the end of the

RSPCA compound some thirty feet from the office, then placed them on the ground and dashed back into the office where I could watch their reactions.

Puppies do not like being left alone, so it was no surprise when one of the youngsters started to whine and run around aimlessly searching for it knew not what and getting nowhere in the process. The other one, however, sat looking around for a few minutes before calmly getting to his feet and heading straight for the office, where he arrived with his tail wagging joyfully.

'So you're the one with the brains,' I said to him, ruffling his coat. 'I could have just the right job for you.'

By now my duties as warden meant I was doing more and more community work for the RSPCA. I was giving more talks than ever, visiting schools and all kinds of social societies, from the WI to youth clubs.

I would give each of them a slide show, demonstrating different aspects of my job, good and bad. It was explicit in showing some of the neglect and cruelty I witnessed on a daily basis. The images of starved rabbits and dogs with overgrown claws drew gasps from the audiences sometimes. I took the view that there was far too much cruelty and abuse going on. Sometimes shock tactics were the only way to get the message across.

Moss, as I christened the collie pup, became my sidekick during these roadshows. He had proved extremely easy to train and had quickly learned to perform all sorts of clever feats at my request. So during my talks he and I would perform little tricks, which proved particularly popular with the children. One favourite involved me very quietly and gently clinking a set of keys in my pocket. The minute I did so Moss would stop what he was doing and come to me.

In the classrooms of the local schools I would encourage the children to play with him. It helped them build a bond with dogs, especially those who were perhaps a little afraid of them. But as they played together in a far corner of the classroom I would give a quiet clink of the keys and Moss would be off, running straight to my side. The children were fascinated by this. They couldn't hear the noise and could never quite work out what had happened.

I had no doubt Moss was a very bright dog, but he proved it to me once and for all at a local agricultural show. A bone had been placed in a bucket full of water, and there was a prize on offer to any dog who would put its head under the water to retrieve the bone.

'Let's have a go,' I said to Moss, showing him the bone lying temptingly at the bottom of the bucket.

Without a second's thought Moss caught hold of the bucket with his teeth, tipped it over and picked up the bone, much to everyone's amusement.

His skills extended way beyond this kind of lateral thinking. As part of my job as warden at the centre, I had to assess a lot of dogs' suitability as pets. It was an important role. The risks of putting a dangerous dog in a family situation were too great to be taken lightly. I also had to assess whether dogs would fit into homes where canines were already present. Moss was my key ally in performing this assessment. He would walk alongside me, just out of reach of the dog that I was leading, ready to jump out of the way should the new dog try to attack him. It helped us spot several dogs that were not going to be good candidates for homes that already had dogs.

Moss was invaluable, too, in catching strays and dogs who were nervous and could not be handled easily off the lead in the compound. He would very cleverly approach the other dog and then stand completely still, allowing it to come to him and sniff around. This gave me the time I needed to quickly use my 'grasper' in the case of a stray or snap a lead on a nervous dog's collar.

Moss also had a talent for helping me catch swans. Given the problems I'd had catching the birds in the past, this proved particularly helpful. If a bird was on a river or large lake, Moss would distract it by lying quietly on the bank within sight of the swan, which would become curious and swim nearer the shore to investigate. This would again give me the split second that I needed to bring my swan hook into play and secure the bird.

Moss's talents became appreciated far and wide.

Every other week Moss would accompany me to the Radio Cornwall studio, lying under the table during the live broadcast devoted to the RSPCA's work in the county. It became something he looked forward to enormously. He always knew the way to the studio down a maze of passages and would run ahead of me to wait outside the correct door.

I often referred to him in the programmes, and after a while listeners began to ask after him, wondering what he had been up to and whether he might visit some event. He became quite the celebrity.

CHAPTER TWENTY-THREE
Teaching a Duck
to Swim

Christmas was only forty-eight hours away, but as I drew
back the curtains in the murky morning light, I already
had a sneaking suspicion my season was once again not going
to be very festive at all.

Outside, the trees were bent double in the gale-force winds
and the rain was pummelling the earth, just as it had done for
two or three days. I couldn't imagine how rough conditions
must be out at sea, but of one thing I was absolutely certain: a
large consignment of oil-soaked birds would be with us very
soon.

265

'Looks like we're going to be in for a busy couple of days. I'd better start ringing round everyone,' I said to Julie, 'before they get too wrapped up in their Christmases.'

The willingness of our team of volunteers to drop everything when crises like this arose was remarkable. Without them, the cleaning centre wouldn't have been able to function. But I still felt a pang of guilt at ringing them a day before Christmas Eve.

I needn't have worried. Each of them agreed to be on standby, indeed most did so in good spirits.

'My turkey's long past saving,' joked one lady who helped us on a regular basis. 'Far better I try and rescue something that's still alive.'

As I'd feared, on Christmas Eve calls reporting the discovery of oiled birds started coming in at the rate of one an hour. Volunteers were soon heading off to collect the blackened and exhausted creatures from the windswept beaches. Soon, scores of them were arriving at the centre.

I noticed immediately that they were almost all guillemots. By evening I realised this was a major incident, but for now, at least, Vicky, Karen, Sue and I could handle the workload. There wasn't any cause to ruin everyone's Christmas just yet.

We always made sure our supplies of cleaning and water-proofing solutions were ready for emergencies like this. Our supplies of frozen sprats were plentiful too. I checked them that evening and could see there was easily enough to ensure the birds got through the Christmas break without going hungry.

By eight o'clock that night, we had set up a series of individual pens, each with an infrared lamp and each capable of taking up to twenty birds. By ten o'clock on Christmas Eve we'd fed and medicated several dozen birds and placed them in their pens. I wished Karen, Sue and Vicky a happy

Christmas, then told them to go home – at least for a few hours.

Christmas morning brought in dozens more birds, these ones even more heavily coated in oil than the previous day's had been. But rather than dragging everyone in, Julie and I enlisted the help of the children. In a funny way, working together to ferry the birds into the cleaning unit, then into their warm pens, we felt as close as any family might do sitting round a table stuffing themselves with turkey. We certainly felt as if we were doing more good.

By Boxing Day well over a hundred birds were installed at the centre. All of them had by now been fed and medicated to help push any ingested oil through the gut. The cleaning hadn't begun yet, however. They needed to rest before the added stress of handling and washing took place.

The more I looked at the guillemots, the more concerned I was becoming for them. Most were underweight, a pretty good indication that they had become contaminated with the oil a long way out at sea. In all likelihood they had been fighting against the pull of the tide for some days before weakness and the rough seas had finally driven them on to the beach. About twenty had already died.

I'd primed Nan and her cleaning team to come in the day after Boxing Day. They arrived to discover around eighty frail-looking birds. For the next couple of days Nan, myself and three other volunteers worked pretty well non-stop.

First we gave the birds their initial wash, removing almost all of the oil. This could take up to twenty minutes for each bird. Afterwards we put them back in the pen to dry out and rest. The following day we gave each bird a second and final wash, removing the last of the oil and leaving the bird clean and hopefully waterproof.

To test this, we put the birds on enclosed pools. But when

we tried this on the third day we discovered, to our horror, that each and every bird wasn't fully waterproof and had to be quickly removed from the water and returned to the indoor pens.

This was disastrous. No matter how carefully one washes oiled birds, there are always one or two that require a further wash. But I had never come across a whole consignment of birds that required a further wash.

We decided to leave things for several days, allowing the birds to rest and then to try again, but it was no use. In desperation I sent off samples of the oil for analysis.

Thanks to the RSPCA, the results were back with us within forty-eight hours. It confirmed my suspicions. The oil contained some kind of wax substance. This explained why it had proven impossible to remove it completely.

There was no known treatment for pollution like this. I asked a few contacts in the RSPCA whether there was anything else we could try, but by now I knew we were faced with only one option.

So it was that, on New Year's Eve, we destroyed all the remaining birds. All of us were left exhausted and deeply depressed by the experience. After all we'd done, it seemed unbelievable that none of the hundred or so birds had made it. It was a bitter blow.

'There was nothing more you could have done,' Julie consoled me that night, echoing the very words I'd delivered to the staff as they'd headed home earlier.

I knew she was right. But it didn't make the sense of failure any easier to bear.

It didn't take long to work out there was something amiss with one of the first arrivals of the New Year.

The brown and black mallard duck had arrived in an

inspector's van that morning. Vicky had taken charge of her and had spent some time checking her out. She was on her way to the waterfowl enclosure with the duck when I spotted them. She'd let the duck have a brief walk. The duck seemed happy enough following her around in the yard, quacking away merrily as she stuck to Vicky's heels. Its reaction to the bantams, pigeons and three peafowl resident in the waterfowl enclosure was altogether different.

The duck boldly walked up to one of the peahens as if she'd never seen another bird before in her life. The peahen was not amused by this overfamiliarity and immediately gave her a sharp peck, which sent the duck scurrying back to me and Vicky.

The duck's reaction to being placed on the pond was even more unusual. Ordinarily this would have eased the nerves of any duck. The sense of being on the water should have made her feel completely at home. Not in this case. The instant I placed the duck on the water she gave out a startled quack and shot out on to the grass where she began preening herself frantically.

'That's a new one,' I said to Vicky. 'A duck that doesn't like the water.'

After placing the duck in a small enclosure where she could get used to other birds without getting into trouble, I headed back to the office to investigate this case a bit further.

The inspector was there completing his paperwork. Talking to him, it was soon pretty plain what had happened. The mallard had been removed from the home of a lady near Newquay. It turned out she had discovered the duck as a duckling, months earlier, on a footpath that skirted round the weed-covered edge of a lake. The bird had been dabbling in the shallow water for an assortment of insects and edible plants and had clearly become separated from her mother.

This wasn't unusual. Mallard ducks are good mothers in so much as they keep their brood warm at night beneath their feathers and find them all the best places to feed. They are also diligent in warning of the dangers of predators like foxes and harriers. Their shrill, alarming quack sets their offspring diving into the reeds until the danger has passed. But, largely because of the threat of predators, they do not suffer stragglers when they take their brood out and about. Ducklings that don't keep up with the rest of the brood get left behind and have to suffer the consequences.

This was almost certainly what had happened in this case. The lost duckling had probably found an extremely interesting patch of mud full of freshwater shrimp and other delicacies and by the time she had eaten her fill the rest of the family had disappeared among the reeds. The duckling had probably cheeped away furiously to no avail.

Whatever the explanation, the duckling had compounded her problems by taking a wrong turning on to a footpath, which was where the lady had found her. Now the correct thing to do in a situation like this is to try to reunite the duckling with its mother. Instead, the lady had been so besotted by the little ball of fluffy down that she had taken her home and kept her as a pet.

She was breaking the law in doing this, of course. To take any wild bird into captivity is an offence. But, either oblivious or unconcerned by this, the lady had kept the bird in her sitting room for the next four months or so. The duckling lived in a cage, where she was well fed and kept clean but had no contact with the outside world.

The results were predictable. The inspector told me that various people had tried to persuade the lady to release the duck, but she had been adamant she was her pet. All the time the duckling had been kept confined in her cage, unable to develop as a bird should. By the time she became a fully grown mallard, the duck had never learned to swim or use her wings.

It was at this point that someone had contacted the RSPCA. The inspector had called and seen that – while the bird's condition was fine – it was living in deeply unsuitable conditions. The lady was also, of course, committing a serious offence.

She hadn't taken kindly to being told this, but after some rather heated words, the inspector had managed to extricate the duck from the home and bring it to the centre.

Obviously there was much that this duck had to learn about life in general, and being a duck in particular. She settled down well enough in the smaller enclosure, eating her corn and seeming content. If I was going to teach her how to do what ducks do best, however, I knew I didn't have much time to waste.

The good news from my point of view was that, being completely tame, the duck was easy to handle. So, a couple of days after her arrival I picked her up and took her back to the pond in the main compound. It was time for this duck to take to water.

Before this could happen, I had to make sure her plumage was waterproof. It was possible that after months of being kept in an unnatural environment, the feathers might have been damaged.

Once more she reacted with horror to the water, darting out and preening herself furiously, just as she had done on her first day with us. Encouragingly, though, I saw that water hadn't penetrated her plumage, so the chances were she was waterproof.

I went through the process again the next day, with more or less the same results. However, as she left the water this time, rather than reacting with panic the duck went through the motions of a bird rather enjoying itself, fluffing up her

271

feathers, lowering her head and shaking her wings. Ordinarily you might expect to see a duck do this on deep water. This one felt more comfortable doing so on grass at the moment, but I felt sure that would change.

This was progress, of sorts, so I decided to build on this over the coming days. The key was reducing the duck's escape options a little. One side of the pond had a steep bank that I knew wouldn't be easy for a duck to scale, so my next step was to put her into the water there. When she found that she could not make her usual quick exit from the pond, the duck sat, floating in one spot, not certain what to do next. It was rather a comic sight. But then gradually her feet began to move as her webs pushed the water behind them.

Slowly but surely, and in a rather crooked and eccentric fashion, she moved out into the centre of the pond. The duck was still uncertain of what to do with her feet and soon headed for shore. As she left the water she stood there looking back at the pond, as if incredulous that she had somehow managed to get to where she now stood. I was delighted, however. The duck had taken a huge step.

Over the coming days the swimming lessons progressed well. Her journeys across the pond became more graceful and less erratic, but she was always quick to get out on to terra firma. Clearly she still thought of this as the place where she felt safest.

Then, one morning, just as she was about to jump out of the pond as usual, the duck found herself confronted by a peacock who had decided to take a drink at the water's edge near her usual disembarkation point. Her early experience had taught her to have a healthy regard for peacocks and their beaks. So the duck turned round in the water and waited, floating quietly while the peacock finished drinking, obviously hoping that once it had done so it would go away.

Unfortunately, having drunk his fill, the peacock lay down on his side alongside the pond and relaxed with one wing spread out, clearly enjoying the morning sun. This sent the duck into a mild panic. She fidgeted around on the water, and then, almost as if she had forgotten herself, flapped her wings violently, sending a shower of water over her body. I held my breath for a moment.

Despite the dislike for water she'd shown so far, I knew that deep down in her DNA, the duck was hard-wired to react to the feel of it on her back. Sure enough, the sensation of being showered triggered the natural urge to bathe that had lain dormant within her for so long.

Within seconds the duck was enjoying a proper bath, splashing around and sending water droplets high into the air. At one point, so much water was thrown into the air some of it fell on the sunbathing peacock. He got up and, adopting the regal demeanour of his species, haughtily walked away from the pond.

That morning marked the turning point for the swimming lessons, and later the same day when I arrived at the compound to feed the birds, I discovered to my delight that the duck was bobbing around happily on the pond. When I threw her corn into a shallow corner, she at once swam across and fed.

I couldn't help smiling broadly. After the trials of Christmas, it was good to feel we could make a difference after all.

CHAPTER TWENTY-FOUR

Summing Up

'It is with much pleasure that I can report a very successful year at the centre.'

It wasn't exactly Stephen King or John Le Carré, but as I read and reread the opening line of the typed script in front of me, I was happy enough with it. What it lacked in page-turning excitement it more than made up for in sincerity, I told myself.

As warden of the Cornish RSPCA Centre, I had to write an annual account of the events there to accompany the annual report of the local branch. I knew the deadline was fast approaching, so this morning I'd sat down and started bashing away at the old iron typewriter in the office.

To my surprise, for once I'd found it easy to write the introductory section. There may have been years in the past when it would have been hard to be so upbeat, but – even allowing for the frustrations of Christmas – 1988, the year on which I was reporting, had genuinely been a good one.

The rest of the account came relatively easily as well, as there was so much to report. In the summer, a mysterious benefactor had given the RSPCA a substantial sum, which had been used to put up a special swan compound. This had come in useful almost immediately when an Australian black swan had been picked up in an exhausted state in Looe Harbour. He'd made a quick recovery in the compound and, as he had never been claimed, had been sent to Newquay Zoo, where he was now in the company of a prospective mate.

By far the most notable change to our procedures had been the introduction of a new home-checking system. The number of dogs, cats and other creatures that had been brought to us from homes that, for one reason or another, could no longer cope with the animal had increased dramatically. Consequently, my colleagues and I had given the matter serious consideration and devised a checking system. This entailed each prospective adoptee being interviewed at home before the pet left the centre. It ensured both the suitability of the home and the compatibility of the selected pet with its prospective owner. The aim was to reduce the chances of animals bouncing back to us only weeks after leaving.

The scheme had come into operation that year, and, to date, eighty volunteers, drawn from the length and breadth of the county, had given up their free time to work as 'home-checkers'. Each had been interviewed at the centre, then sent out with an experienced checker who showed them the ropes. Provided they were deemed up to it, they were then given ID cards.

The whole set-up was monitored by a coordinator, Joe Morris, who did a fantastic job keeping records and making certain that the system worked efficiently. (It was in fact working extremely well. There was already talk of it being tried out in other counties around the country.)

More than ever this year, we were grateful for the help of a group of outsiders. These ranged from the local vets and newspaper editors who had done much to spread the word of our work, to the team at Newquay Zoo, who had helped us out with the rehoming of several exotic animals. Last, and certainly not least, I remembered to pay a small tribute in my annual account to Julie, or as I'd described her 'my long suffering wife, who never knows what time to expect me for meals or what creature will be sharing our home next'. It was the least I could do given what I put her through every year, I told myself.

Having read the introduction over for the umpteenth time, I was satisfied with the written report, but I felt it needed something more, so I decided to give it some real authority by putting in hard figures about the numbers of animals we'd treated that year.

I'd never really had the time, or indeed the inclination, to sit down and do an inventory of the animals that had passed through our portals. I rummaged through the files and found the diary and logs that we now kept diligently. When I started totting up the numbers, I couldn't quite believe the figures taking shape in front of me.

That year, for instance, we'd handled an unbelievable 638 cats and kittens. As I looked at the log recording dog arrivals, I saw that we'd had 186 dogs and puppies too. Birds, as usual, had been the most numerous visitors. That year 1,082 winged creatures had been treated. The number was made up of the usual A to Z of avian life, from an Amazon parrot to some zebra finches. Of the 150 miscellaneous other species we'd taken in that year, the most unusual were the long-eared bats that had been discovered when workmen opened up a roof in St Agnes. They'd been an interesting addition to the centre for the few weeks they'd been with us.

I put each category down in a table. When I totted up all the animals for that year, the total came to 2,056. For a moment or two I sat there staring into space.

Two thousand and fifty six, I laughed to myself. How on earth did we manage that?

Having started playing with figures, I persisted. I grabbed a calculator and did a simple sum. It turned out we'd been treating more than five animals a day every day for a year. This set me thinking about how many animals we must have treated here at Ferndale. And how many more had we looked after during our days at the Rosery?

OK, let's assume two thousand a year for the past five years, one and a half thousand for the fifteen years before that and a thousand a year for the ten years before that, I said to myself.

I tapped the numbers into the calculator and leaned back in my chair. The figure was too long to make any sense to me whatsoever.

I hadn't noticed Julie arriving in the office.

'Oh, hello, have a look at that,' I said, handing her the piece of paper with the figures jotted down on it.

'What's this, your new salary?' she joked.

'As if,' I laughed. 'No, that's the number of animals I reckon we've treated since we started taking them in back at the Rosery.'

'What?' she said, looking intently at the piece of paper once more. 'Are you sure? That can't be right, can it?'

'Here're the sums,' I said. 'We've had more than two

thousand this year and we've been going for nearly thirty years.'

Julie slowly tapped in the figures herself. When the figure came up exactly the same as mine, she raised her eyebrows and simply said, 'Gosh.' Soon she too was sitting down shaking her head quietly to herself, lost in her own thoughts. I'm sure they mirrored my own.

The days when we'd first dreamed of starting a small animal sanctuary together seemed part of another era, another world in fact. In the decades since then we had watched those dreams come to life, haphazardly, almost accidentally on some occasions. Along the way we'd shared moments of frustration and fulfilment, happiness and heartbreak. But slowly, with the backing of the RSPCA and the help of some wonderful friends, it had happened. And now, here we were, hosting Cornwall's only official RSPCA animal centre, running a professional operation that, at times, resembled a small military unit. It defied belief, really.

Not once, however, had Julie and I sat down and thought about the scale of what we'd done or the journey we'd undertaken. But, then, why would we have? We were only doing what we had always wanted to do, helping creatures unable to help themselves, providing a second chance for animals, many of whom had suffered at the hands of humans. Besides, even if we'd wanted to take stock in that way, life was simply too busy. We'd never had the time to dwell on such things.

And we still didn't.

The loud ringing of the phone snapped us both out of our spells.

Julie took the call, and her voice was soon taking on a serious tone. She listened for a few moments, then asked the caller to hold on.

'Woman over in Perranporth,' she said sotto voce, cupping

her hand over the mouthpiece. 'Just picked up an injured buzzard.'

'OK,' I said. 'Tell her to bring it over. Let's see what we can do.'

Keeping Animals – Some Do's and Don'ts

Dogs

Before you decide to buy a puppy, do a bit of research to find out the breed that would best suit your lifestyle. Remember, a dog's lifespan is usually at least twelve years. That's twelve years of commitment, which will include veterinary expenses, boarding fees and of course, most importantly, your time, to exercise, train and groom.

There are a few important do's and don'ts:

- Don't buy a dog if you are out at work all day. Four hours alone is about the maximum time for a dog to be left alone.

- Don't buy a particular breed on impulse. It may look very beautiful, but ask yourself why that breed was developed and then whether you can provide the sort of life that would suit it.
- Don't ever think of a dog as a little human being. A dog is a dog; it does not benefit from overindulgence, but thrives on sensible attention and training. Remember, dogs make wonderful friends and servants but terrible masters!
- Do take your puppy to training classes.
- Do talk to your dog. Believe it or not, many dog owners seem to find this difficult unless they are giving orders.

Cats

There are so many different breeds of cat to choose from these days. If you are thinking of taking on a kitten, get out a book from the library and read up about the cats that take your fancy. If possible, visit a breeder and find out the requirements of that particular breed. As with dogs, there are some do's and don'ts:

- Don't buy a beautiful fluffy kitten such as a Persian unless you are prepared to groom the cat each and every day. The Persian coat gets matted very easily, and neglect for even a few days can cause real problems. If you accidentally hurt the cat when trying to untangle the knots, he will no longer trust you when you advance holding a brush and comb and will become difficult to groom. This may well result in a regular visit to the vet's to be groomed, or clipped, under sedation.
- Don't shut your cat out of the house when you are at work. There are too many possible dangers. If you

cannot provide a cat flap, then leave the cat indoors with a litter tray. He will be safe then.

- Don't feel that you have to buy two kittens as company for each other. Cats are by nature loners; although they will tolerate other cats in their household, they are probably happier to be the only one.
- Don't insist on buying a pedigree cat. Remember, an ordinary domestic cat can be just as rewarding as a pet.

Rabbits

Rabbits have always been considered the ideal children's pet. But the fact is that they are not as suitable as they appear when you first see them as cute, fluffy baby bunnies in the pet-shop window. Before deciding on buying one as a pet, I strongly advise that you contemplate the pros and cons:

- A carefully handled rabbit, particularly a male, can with luck remain amenable to being picked up and petted, even as an adult. But once past the baby stage many rabbits resent being handled, and does in particular can become quite savage when they reach breeding age. Rabbits have extremely sharp teeth and claws and can inflict pretty nasty wounds. Should a child get bitten a couple of times, the pet's appeal will quickly fade to be replaced by a sense of fear.
- In general the larger breeds such as the New Zealand white make better pets, temperament-wise, than the smaller varieties, but for a single pet always choose a male.
- Two rabbits brought up together can be good company for each other but they should be spayed or neutered.
- Provide as large a hutch as possible, ideally with an outside run, and position the hutch so that it is out of the

full strength of the summer sun and sheltered from icy winds and rain in winter.

- Don't buy a long-haired rabbit unless you are prepared for endless grooming. On the whole Angoras and Kashmirs are unsuitable as pets and require specialist accommodation.
- Provide a varied diet and, very importantly, make sure the rabbit's living quarters are cleaned out frequently.

Guinea Pigs

The inoffensive and ever attractive guinea pig is probably one of the best pets for children past the age of five or six.

The only problem is that they are not too easy for little hands to hold, as they can squirm and wriggle, so a guinea pig should always be handled close to the ground in case it falls and injures its back.

Other useful points to consider:

- Guinea pigs hate cold and damp, so it is advisable to keep their hutch in the shelter of a garage or shed during the winter months.
- A portable hutch and run is ideal accommodation in the summer, when the guinea pigs will enjoy doing the lawnmowing for you!
- Guinea pigs are highly sociable and several can be kept together, but make certain that they are all the same sex unless you want a population explosion . . .

Tame Rats and Mice

Some do's and don'ts for your pet rat or mouse:

- Handle your pet rat as often as you can and it will keep tame and trusting.

- Give your pet as large a cage as possible with toys and bits of cardboard and wood to chew.
- Tame mice urinate when being handled, so make sure you wash your hands well after you have been picking them up.
- Don't feed meat or cheese to rats or mice.
- Watch out for your mouse or rat's safety when you have it running loose in a room. You can be certain your cat will also be watching carefully for a different reason!

Hamsters and Gerbils

- Most pet hamsters have cages that are too small for their nocturnal activities, so get one as large as possible and provide interesting things like old toilet rolls and chunks of wood to keep your pet occupied.
- Large fish tanks make ideal homes for both hamsters and gerbils. Gerbils enjoy digging in sand or peat, which can be spread thickly over the floor of the tank.
- Hamsters sleep deeply through the day and should not be disturbed too abruptly. Sudden handling may result in the handler getting bitten.
- Hamsters are solitary animals and it is unwise to keep more than one in a cage; gerbils are more sociable and can live in groups but, like guinea pigs, make sure they are all of the same sex or your happy group of five can quickly become two dozen.

Budgerigars

Male budgies make the best pets if you want one to become finger-tame and perhaps learn to talk. The younger the budgie, the easier it is to tame.

Here are some more pointers:

- Do buy as large a cage as you can afford, and avoid the fancy, overly ornamental types in favour of a straight-forward model that is as long as possible, to allow the bird to exercise properly.
- Don't clutter the inside of the cage with too many toys.
- Budgies are sociable birds so ensure that your pet's cage is kept in a room where it can see all that is going on, but beware of placing the cage near a window or where there is the possibility of fumes from a gas fire or cooker.
- Budgies enjoy being let out of their cages to fly around the room, but first ensure that all the windows are closed, the door shut and the fireplace covered.
- Don't forget to provide green food. Clean dandelion leaves or chickweed are best. Lettuce is a poor substitute.

Canaries

Only male canaries sing, although some females do some-times have a go. Some breeds have pretty loud voices so go for the quieter varieties like glosters, Fifes or rollers. Rollers have specially trained songs, which consist of a series of trills.

- Buy your canary as large a cage as possible. Avoid the fancy types in favour of a basic model. Buy a long cage to allow the bird to exercise properly.
- For some reason, bird cages fitted with wooden perches nearly always have a round dowel for the perches. Canaries and finches are more comfortable resting on perches with flat tops, so pop the round dowel in a vice and plane down the top; your pet's feet will certainly benefit.
- Canaries do not usually become as tame as budgies, but with patience some can become finger-tame.
- Don't place your pet's cage in direct sunlight or

anywhere where there are fumes from gas fires or cookers.

- Remember to provide green food. As with budgies, dandelion and chickweed are best.

Peacocks

Don't try keeping peacocks unless you can give them their freedom or have an extensive aviary; you will also need tolerant neighbours who can put up with the incessant screaming of the male birds during the breeding season (late April to July).

- If your peafowl are confined, they will benefit from extra protein when moulting; raw mince, cheap tinned dog food and cheese are ideal substitutes for the insects that they would be eating if they had free range.
- Peahens are best confined in aviaries when breeding. All too often foxes will take both eggs and hen if the peahen has nested at liberty.
- Pea chicks are best reared on turkey starter crumbs and should be kept well away from poultry as they have very little immunity and can pick up diseases easily.
- Peacock males are three years old before they grow their full train.

Parrots, Cockatoos and Macaws

Think carefully before you take a parrot into your home. They are demanding pets that hate isolation, can be extremely noisy and will possibly outlive you!

African grey parrots are great mimics, but usually one-person birds. Blue-fronted and yellow-fronted Amazon parrots make good family pets and talkers. Cockatoos are the most sensitive of the parrot family; they are noisy, active birds and can become extremely tame with their owners and demand constant attention. They are easily stressed by being left alone in an empty room, and some turn to self-destruction and chew up or pull out their feathers. Hand-reared macaws make wonderful pets if you have the time and the space for them and can put up with their raucous voices.

Here are some more tips:

- The largest cage available should be the aim, especially in the case of cockatoos, which need space to climb around and to exercise their wings.
- Never use metal perches; wooden perches will almost certainly be chewed up, but this is part of the parrot's natural behaviour and should not be stopped. Keep a store of replacements.
- Remove the metal grid on the bottom of the parrot's cage and allow the bird to walk on the flat tray.
- Always buy an English-bred parrot. You may pay more for it, but imported birds are often caught wild and may never become tame.

Wild Birds

It is a sad fact that hundreds of garden birds are dying as the result of picking up infection from dirty bird tables and unwashed drinkers. Here are some do's and don'ts:

- Bird tables and drinkers should ideally be cleaned every day and all seed husks and uneaten food removed.
- Summer feeding should be reduced to allow birds to forage for their natural foods.
- Clean out nestboxes in the autumn, removing old nests and reducing the build-up of parasites.

Bird Casualties

If you find an injured bird, take it to a rescue centre or to a veterinary practice but, in the latter case, make certain that the vet understands wild birds. Many do not.

If you find a baby bird, provided it has feathers, pick it up carefully and place it in a thick bush or hedge nearby and then leave it alone. In most cases it is not lost and its parents are not far away, but they will not come to feed their offspring if you stand around watching.

Chickens

The idea of keeping a few chickens in the back garden has become popular once more. Most people are attracted by the prospect of fresh eggs; others take on 'fancier' breeds as pets and even for competition purposes.

On the whole, chickens aren't difficult to maintain, but a few points are worth thinking about:

- Do decide from the start what breed of chicken would suit your purposes. There are hundreds of different breeds, in all shapes and sizes. One of the best ways to find out about them is to visit a large poultry show and ask advice from the exhibitors. There are also several good books on poultry.
- Do make sure your poultry have good-sized accommodation and never overcrowd them. Poultry houses and arks are not cheap to buy, so make certain that the one you choose is large enough to house the number of hens you intend to keep. You don't want to be buying newer, bigger homes all the time.
- Do also make sure that the home is easy to clean, has sufficient ventilation and, very importantly, has perches that can easily be removed for cleaning.

- Do keep your poultry house clean. Scrape out the bird droppings at least once a week and, most importantly, take out the perches to check for the presence of red mite, a tiny parasite that lives on the end of perches and in cracks in the woodwork by day and emerges at night to suck the blood of the roosting hens. Red mite are responsible for many deaths in domestic poultry. Sprays can be obtained that will help keep these pests at bay.
- Don't keep poultry without checking whether your local council allows it. Many do not.
- Don't keep a cockerel unless you have very tolerant neighbours who do not object to being woken up at dawn by his crowing.

Pigeons and Doves

A lot of people get confused about these two – which isn't surprising. The white birds we keep in dovecotes are usually referred to as doves, although in fact they are really pigeons. Woodpigeons, on the other hand, are also called ring doves. No wonder people get into a pickle.

The good news, however, is that whichever of these birds you choose, they are among the easiest avian pets to keep. Here are a few do's and don'ts:

- Do place your dovecotes on walls. Cotes mounted on walls ensure the birds are safer from predators such as sparrow hawks. Placing the dovecote as high as possible also protects the birds from the very real threat presented by cats.
- If you do go for a free-standing dovecote, it should be as large as possible and provide two pigeon holes for each pair of pigeons. It should also be situated in a position

where it is reasonably sheltered from northerly and easterly winds.

- Do choose dovecotes that can be easily cleaned. Many manufactured dovecotes look beautiful but they don't allow for the fact that pigeons are messy birds and their cote will need frequent cleaning. When buying a dove-cote, ensure that you can get your hand and a scraper into the individual pigeon holes with ease. Don't allow the pigeon holes to become clogged with droppings.
- Don't allow your birds to over-produce. Pigeons breed all the year round and in no time at all your dovecote could be overflowing. To prevent this, newly laid eggs should be removed and replaced with plastic or china pigeon eggs. The birds will be oblivious to the difference and will try to incubate these instead.
- To help prevent disease, feed the pigeons away from the dovecote, preferably in containers that can be easily cleaned and get rid of stale food.
- Do provide a container of clean water so that the birds can bathe.